DISPOSED OF
BY LIBRARY
HOUSE OF LORDS

ILLEGAL IMMIGRANTS AND DEVELOPMENTS IN EMPLOYMENT IN THE LABOUR MARKETS OF THE EU

DAMES

Dansk Center for Migration
og Etniske Studier

**EUROPEAN RESEARCH CENTRE
ON MIGRATION & ETHNIC RELATIONS**

Illegal Immigrants and Developments in Employment in the Labour Markets of the EU

JAN HJARNØ
Danish Centre for Migration and Ethnic Studies
University of Southern Denmark

ASHGATE

© Jan Hjarnø 2003

All rights reserved. No part of this publication may be reproduced, stored in a retrieval system or transmitted in any form or by any means, electronic, mechanical, photocopying, recording or otherwise without the prior permission of the publisher.

Published by
Ashgate Publishing Limited
Gower House
Croft Road
Aldershot
Hampshire GU11 3HR
England

Ashgate Publishing Company
Suite 420
101 Cherry Street
Burlington, VT 05401-4405
USA

Ashgate website: http//:www.ashgate.com

British Library Cataloguing in Publication Data
Hjarnø, Jan
  Illegal immigrants and developments in employment in the
  labour markets of the EU. - (Research in migration and
  ethnic relations series)
  1.Illegal aliens - Employment - European Union countries
  2.Alien labor - European Union countries 3.Labor market -
  European Union countries
  I.Title
  331.6'2'094

Library of Congress Control Number: 2001097969

ISBN 0 7546 1688 6

Printed and bound in Great Britain by MPG Books Ltd, Bodmin, Cornwall

Contents

List of Figures

List of Tables

Acknowledgement

Shortly before Christmas 1995 Dr. Joan Ramakers, Hoger Instituut voor de Arbeid, Leuven asked me to participate in a seminar in Brussels, 18-19 January 1996, on undocumented immigrants on the labour markets of the European Union. Before I received his call I had never paid any attention to undocumented immigrants in the labour market in Denmark because we don't have illegal labour immigrants in the labour market. He called my attention to the problem, and I no longer have any doubts that the very fact that we have none may be of relevance to understanding the factors governing the presence or non-presence of illegal immigrants. I am therefore very grateful to Dr. Joan Ramakers for making me aware of the phenomenon, which compelled me to look more closely into the matter and produce this book.

To my research assistant, Mr. Torben Jensen, I owe more than can be expressed in a few words. His knowledge, advice and suggestions were invaluable. He has checked all the figures and tables, and I am extremely obliged to him for all his labour. I also wish to thank my colleague at the Danish Centre for Migration and Ethnic Studies Dr. John Wrench, senior lecturer Steen Scheuer, Copenhagen School of Economics and senior lecturer Jens Lind, University of Aalborg. Their advice and co-operation have been indispensable. Further I wish to thank Mrs. Jackie Langelund and Mr. David Clayre, M.Sc. (Lond.), who corrected my English, translated parts of the manuscript and edited my far from tidy manuscript. Finally I also wish to thank our secretary, Mrs. Ulla Oehlenschläger, for preparing the manuscript for printing.

To all who made this study possible, I convey my warmest thanks.

Jan Hjarnø
Director of Research - Danish Centre for Migration and Ethnic Studies
Esbjerg

Jan Hjarnø, Director of the Danish Centre for Migration and Ethnic Studies, died suddenly in Autumn 2002 and did not live to see the printed book. He was a pioneer in Denmark in the academic study of migration and ethnic relations, and the book stands as a testament to his extensive and unique contribution to this field of study.

1 Introduction

In 1993, Professor D. S. North wrote in an OECD report that governments in democratic countries would never be able to solve the problem of illegal immigration precisely because they are democratic countries. "In a sense, the struggle over immigration policy is like a struggle over environmental policy; the narrowly focused opponents of immigration enforcement, along with their diverse allies, like the narrowly focused opponents of pollution, have much more at stake than those on the other side of the issue. Reducing acid rain is probably a good idea for society as a whole, but no individuals or institutions will benefit quickly in any tangible way. However, reducing acid rain will, quickly and tangibly hurt a number of specific interests. Similarly, effective immigration enforcement will bring major losses to certain narrow interest groups but no immediate tangible benefits to any broader groups."[1] For this simple reason, therefore, democratic governments, according to North, will lack the willpower to apply the economic, diplomatic and intellectual resources necessary to implement a totally effective restriction of illegal labour immigration.

This is not correct. There are at least four democratic countries in which governments have experienced no difficulty in solving the problem of illegal labour immigrants: Denmark, Norway, Finland and Sweden. Apart from Finland,[2] these four countries have not practised a more restrictive immigration policy than most other countries in the EU, but there are still practically very few illegal labour immigrants.

The purpose of this book is to answer the question:

Why are there hardly any illegal immigrants in the labour markets in the Nordic countries?

As a starting point I will begin with a short story from real life:

I recently met a friend who grows tomatoes. When I asked how he was doing, he said it was difficult to make a living because his competitors in Holland used low-paid illegal immigrants to pick the crop. He said: "Don't imagine the Dutch tomato you had at lunch was picked and caressed by a blue-eyed, blonde, big-breasted Dutch girl in clogs. It was more likely picked and packed by a thin, underpaid, dark-haired, frightened Tamil who had his application for political asylum turned down long ago, and who has survived since by working illegally in Holland. You will find him and a couple of other Tamils living very primitively near the greenhouse boiler. If the Dutch authorities learn of their presence, they would ask the employer to send them away and, if he agrees, he would not normally be punished. The Dutch authorities are more interested in protecting employers' ability to compete, and in Dutch tomato exports, than they are in punishing producers who exploit poor illegal Tamil labourers." My response was: "Why don't you get yourself a couple of Tamils who have been refused political asylum and who would be happy to work for a fraction of what you pay a Danish labourer?" He replied: "If I followed your advice I would be approached in no time by the foreman of the local trade union, who would tell me to lay them off immediately or he would blockade my production, report me to the Employers Association and file a case against me in the Labour Court. He could put me out of business without any trouble, and I could not expect any understanding or support from the Employers Association. My peers would consider me a pariah and ostracise me mercilessly. I wouldn't dare employ an illegal immigrant. Comparing the risk with the possible profit, it is just not worth it."

I do not know if my friend's story about the Dutch tomatoes is true,[3] but I know that illegal immigrants are at work in most countries in the EU: Italy, Greece, Spain, Portugal, Austria, France, Belgium, Germany and Holland.[4] The international labour organisation, ILO, has estimated that the number of illegal immigrants working in the member countries of the Council of Europe is 2.6 million.[5] The phenomenon of illegal labour immigrants is practically unknown in Denmark, Sweden, Norway and Finland, and this absence is not due to the lack of an informal economy with a market for illegal labour. Like most countries in Europe, the Scandinavian ones also have an informal economy and a market for illegal labour, but there are hardly any illegal labour immigrants.[6]

The case of my tomato-growing friend indicates that there are apparently two ways of preventing illegal labour immigrants. In Holland it seems to be the State authorities that inspect and control employers, whereas in Denmark my friend did not dare employ illegal immigrants because he feared the response by the unions and his own colleagues in the Employers Association. We can thus differentiate between State control, as in Holland, and a control carried out by the social partners, the trade unions and the employers' associations, as in Denmark.

Definitions and analytical framework

I will define "illegal labour migration" as the process whereby foreign nationals enter a country and take up work there without a labour permit. "Illegal labour immigrants" are thus defined as foreign nationals working in a country without a labour permit. In many cases illegal labour immigrants are also individuals who have no legal residence permit, but there are exceptions. Individuals who enter a country as tourists usually have the legal right to remain for up to three months, and it is only if they take up work without a labour permit that they can be classified as illegal immigrants.

A precondition for illegal labour migration is that a market exists for illegal labour, requires the qualifications offered by illegal labour immigrants, and employers who are prepared to take the risk of employing foreigners illegally. The phenomenon of illegal labour immigration also requires that there are foreigners ready to take work without a legal labour permit. There are plenty of such people in the countries outside the European Union, and in my opinion one cannot blame people suffering from unemployment and poverty for attempting to get a job illegally in an EU country. On the contrary, one should direct one's attention to the employers. The fact is that there would be no illegal labour immigrants if there were no employers to employ them.

The primary focus of research into the phenomenon of illegal labour immigration is therefore to disclose the factors, which cause employers to decide to take on illegal labour immigrants. A study comparing the Nordic EU countries with the rest of the EU can explain the differences in the use of illegal immigrants.

I do not believe the differences between employers' use of illegal labour immigrants in the different countries of the EU is due to fundamental differences in moral and ethical attitudes to the question of using illegal labour. Employers all over the world employ people in order to make a profit. Whether or not an employer takes on illegal immigrants is based on a rational choice. If employers estimate that the risk of using illegal immigrants is low compared to the increased profit they will consider using illegal immigrants, and some will actually employ them.[7]

In order to understand the phenomenon of illegal labour immigration, we must analyse the situation in the labour market in relation to the risks the individual employer runs in employing illegal immigrants compared to the possible benefits gained by employing them on substandard pay and conditions. It is also necessary to analyse developments in the demand for labour. This demand can vary over time, and in Denmark the demand for the type of qualifications offered by illegal immigrants has declined. Finally, it seems important in this context to analyse the way in which labour is recruited. In certain circumstances, this factor may create insurmountable barriers against the employment of illegal labour immigrants.

Illegal labour immigration only occurs 1) if there is a market for the type of qualifications offered by the illegal immigrants, and 2) if there are employers who estimate the risk times the penalty for employing illegal immigrants as minor compared with the economic advantages of violating the law by employing them.

A precondition for the existence of illegal labour immigration is the existence of an informal economy. By this I mean the non-declared part of the market economy - i.e. the sale, or the production for sale (or exchange), of goods and services without declaration of the transaction or income to the relevant authorities. In relation to illegal labour immigrants, special interest will be attached to those non-declared activities which have a lower-than-normal price, agreed on by the buyer and seller in the knowledge of the non-declaration in order to share the savings made in taxes, duties, etc. These activities are termed "black".

It is a widely held assumption that the proportion of illegal activities in a country is closely related to taxes and duties.[8] High taxation leads to declaration of expenditure and reticence in declaring income. If taxes and duties increase, illegal activities also increase. However, this assumption does not apply in all circumstances. The extent of the informal economy in relation to the gross national product fluctuates for a number of reasons, and the demand for labour is subject to variations related to structural changes in the economy.[9]

One of the major tasks of research into the prevention of the employment of illegal labour immigrants is, therefore, to study the risks involved, including an analysis of possible control and penalty mechanisms, and the value of the performance given by the illegal immigrants.

Organisation of the study

Since the purpose of establishing the European Union was to create one large, common market with free movement of capital, goods and labour, and since the use of illegal immigrants creates barriers to this free movement, I have let my study of illegal labour immigrants in the EU take its starting point here. The present work starts, therefore, by presenting a number of recent analyses of the movement of labour within the EU. A common factor in these analyses is that the theoretical models used do not tally with the empirical findings. In order to explain these differences, researchers have referred to various historical conditions, which have not been included in the theoretical models, and the validity of which they have not tested. This results in uncertainty as to the validity of their explanations, and it is necessary to extend the theories to take account of historical factors thought to influence the free movement of labour on EU markets.

In an attempt to create such a theoretical extension, I have taken as my starting point the changes in the international division of labour currently taking place as a result of the restructuring of the global economy. This restructuring has noticeably affected conditions in the labour markets of the EU and North America. Throughout the major industrial centres in Europe and North America, there has been a fall in employment in industry, which to a large extent has moved to areas with lower wage costs. As a result of this de-industrialisation, unemployment has risen in many of the former industrial centres, but at the same time restructuring has led to a demand for a highly developed, specialised business service sector built on the ruins of the former industrial centres and creating employment not only for highly- trained specialists but also for the many who in varying ways service these specialists through cleaning, transportation, hotels, restaurants, etc. These services are often routine functions, making no specific demands on the educational qualifications of the workforce.

As a consequence of restructuring, the trade unions in many countries have lost their political power, resulting in pay and working conditions being controlled by purely economic market forces to a greater extent than before. In many of the former industrial countries this has led to the disintegration of pay and working conditions for those employed in the simple, routine production of services. An extremely low-paid labour market has arisen, especially employing people discriminated against in normal job-seeking because of their sex, skin-colour or linguistic abilities. That is why there are many women, coloureds and immigrants in this new, extremely low-paid area in the service sector. This development has taken place in a number of former centres such as New York and London, but it does not apply to conditions in, for instance, Copenhagen. In many ways Copenhagen has experienced a development similar to that in New York and London, but it has not led to the formation of an extremely low-paid area in the service sector.

A review of a number of new theories concerning social differentiation seems to give no valid explanation of the difference in development between New York and Copenhagen. Many of the theories advanced in recent years are characterised by the view that the classic theories and concepts concerning social differentiation are out-of-date and cannot be used because conditions have changed since they were created. These assertions are not documented. Capitalism has not been abolished, even though many of the former capitalist industrial centres are now in a so-called post-modern phase in which the service sector has become dominant. The concepts which Marx used in his analysis of the development of capitalism in the nineteenth century are still applicable in the attempt to explain developments in the current capitalist labour markets.

In these labour markets one sees an increasingly extreme polarisation between functions requiring a high level of training and specialisation of the labour force, and simple routine functions requiring low educational and specialist qualifications. The market demands two different types of employees: the career-minded, and those who are just interested in having a job, which does not require a high level of education.

My hypothesis is that a modern economy requires four kinds of social actors: 1) investors wishing to invest in production to achieve maximisation of their capital; 2) actors wishing to educate themselves in order to make a career as highly trained specialists; 3) actors to carry out simple, routine work not requiring a high level of educational qualifications, and 4) actors wishing to start their own businesses because independence is their aim in life.

Actors with these differing ways of life have existed for a long time, and contemporary social actors have been influenced during their childhood and adolescence by the lifestyle practised by their parents and close relatives. Contemporary social actors are thus characterised by various norms and values, which affect their actions, leading to actors with different lifestyles, can be expected to act differently if they end up in the same social situation and have the possibility for action. Thus their reactions to unemployment may be expected to vary.

Before this supposition can be tested it is necessary to understand the causes of the unemployment, which has arisen in the former industrial centres, and what possibilities social actors with different ways of life offer for action. As a basis for the analysis, conditions in Denmark have been chosen. Here, researchers agree that unemployment is a problem, but opinions polarise as soon as the possible causes are discussed. At one pole are the neo-liberal sociologists and economists who focus particularly on the supply side. Their analyses therefore build on a very narrow perspective that results amongst other things in their believing in the necessity for the creation of greater differentiation in pay-levels. By lowering the level of pay for certain types of work they believe that a foundation can be created for lower production costs, and thereby greater competitiveness, resulting in higher employment. These researchers fail to take account of the fact that unemployment is not just a question of a labour glut on the market but also of lack of demand. At the other pole are those who apply a broader perspective and do not believe that a fall in pay will necessarily increase the competitiveness of Danish labour internationally, thereby creating a fertile basis for higher employment and greater economic growth in the long-term. Despite high levels of pay, a high rate of unemployment and high social payments to the unemployed, Denmark has managed well compared with many other former industrial countries. Danish production is competitive on an international level, and the solution to unemployment must be found in a reclassification of the unemployed, from the socially stigmatising role as unemployed to roles that are not socially stigmatising, such as persons taking early retirement, persons on child-minding or educational leave, and so on.

As long as one restricts oneself to looking at developments in the Danish labour market alone, it can be difficult to obtain solid, convincing documentation as to which of the two research groups is right. It is therefore necessary to compare developments in Denmark with developments in a country where the neo-liberal researchers' suggestions have been tried out. In the USA a neo-liberal strategy has been practised for many years, and market forces have to a great extent been allowed to solve unemployment. The comparison shows that, despite the costs of high levels of pay, a significant level of unemployment, and a heavy burden of public relief payments with correspondingly high levels of taxation, Denmark has managed to reach higher levels of productivity and a higher per capita production than the USA. The comparison documents that the high level of Danish social welfare, which includes greater equality of income, promotes this economic growth. Other researchers have reached the same conclusion, based on a number of new international studies on the relationship between economic growth and developments in income distribution. The Danish labour policy that has been implemented has thus, as far as economic growth is concerned, been beneficial to Denmark, and the high level of unemployment is not so much an economic problem as a problem of social classification. Too many Danes end up in the socially stigmatising role of unemployed, despite political efforts at reclassification through socially non-stigmatising programmes such as early retirement, parental leave and educational leave.

Developments in Danish industry are affected by the fact that the social actors have different lifestyles. Actors who have been influenced throughout their the childhood and adolescence by an independent lifestyle as self-employed will be more likely to try to establish themselves as selfemployed than those who have been influenced by a careerist or wage earning lifestyle. The conditions for establishing oneself as self-employed have changed. Decentralisation of higher education and developments within transport and communication have given entrepreneurs greater opportunities for establishing themselves outside the former industrial centres, and many entrepreneurs in the manufacturing sector have taken advantage of these opportunities. The majority of new jobs in the manufacturing sector arise in rural areas, while the former urban industrial centres are experiencing a fall in employment in the manufacturing sector. At the same time as employment in the manufacturing sector has fallen, there has been a growth in employment in the business service sector. This development has created a demand for a number of service functions that do not require highly qualified labour. Many small independent firms have appeared in the service sector in the form of small shops, restaurants, transport firms, cleaning companies, etc., which have immigrants and refugees as entrepreneurs. The former migration of Danish entrepreneurs from rural areas to the large urban centres is being supplanted by refugees and immigrants.

When Denmark imported labour at the end of the 1960s the majority of the foreign workers went into the manufacturing sector in the former centres. Many of the companies that employed them have now disappeared or have reduced their workforce, so that many immigrants have become unemployed, which is a heavy burden. The prevalence of entrepreneurs amongst immigrants and refugees is highest in those groups in which the majority have their roots in rural communities, where they grew up in families who were independently self-employed, while the frequency is lowest in groups who performed industrial work in their homelands. Much seems to suggest that lifestyle plays a role in the desire to be an entrepreneur and has provided experience as to how a business can be started and run.

A prerequisite for the employment of illegal immigrants is the existence of an informal labour market. Such a market exists in all countries, but the need for labour may vary greatly from country to country. In some places there is a need for the qualifications that illegal immigrants can offer; in other places, the demand is of such a character and recruitment organised in such a way as to discourage the use of illegal immigrants. The demand for the type of labour which illegal immigrants can offer is, for instance, very limited in Denmark, because a large part of the work requires occupational qualifications possessed by but a few immigrants and refugees. Moreover, recruitment of labour for the informal labour market mainly takes place through closed, social networks to which few immigrants and refugees have access. The need for illegal labour immigrants is therefore limited in Denmark.

However, the main reason that there are hardly any illegal immigrants in the labour markets in Denmark, Sweden and Finland is not a lack of demand for this type of labour, but that labour markets in the Nordic countries are organised in such a way that employers are prevented from employing illegal immigrants. In the Nordic countries there is highly developed democracy in the labour market, controlled by collective agreements that provide norms for pay and working conditions, also for employers who are not members of professional organisations. Under this system, the embargo on strikes and lock-outs is wide-reaching, and employers trying to break agreements by employing illegal immigrants know that they will rapidly meet sanctions from both the employers' and the employees' side. Employers, therefore, eschew this kind of violation of the law. In other EU countries, collective bargaining plays a minor role, and it is not the parties within the labour market who direct and control conditions in the labour market. The State plays a major role and tries to ensure amongst other things that foreigners lacking labour permits are not employed. There are many disadvantages connected with such State control. It is expensive, and the presence of the many illegal labour immigrants demonstrates that the control is ineffective and that employers regard the employment of illegal immigrants as economically advantageous.

To illustrate empirical conditions in the labour markets in the EU, we can look at empirical descriptions of conditions in Portugal, Germany and Denmark. For decades Portugal has been an exporter of labour, with extremely low pay levels and weak trade unions. Since the country's entry into the EU, foreign capital has flowed in from those wishing to exploit the low levels of pay, and capital has come from the EU to develop the infrastructure. This resulted in a shortage of labour in, for instance, the building and installation sector, which has again created pressure for wage increases. To counteract this, Portugal allowed the importation of labour from a number of former colonies. Part of this importation takes place illegally, and a significant proportion of the immigrant labour force is illegal. Documentation exists that illegal labour immigrants are exposed to gross exploitation in the form of under-payment and wretched working conditions. The Portuguese trade union movement is weak and is reluctant to report employers hiring illegal immigrants. The reason given for this reluctance is the fear that reporting them will result in deportation of the illegal immigrants. These illegal immigrants have thus created a dilemma for the Portuguese trade union movement. It can either choose to report the employers hiring illegal immigrants, which will result in them being deported and insignificant fines for the employers. Alternatively it can choose, as it has done, not to report them and try instead to have the illegal immigrants recognised as legal immigrants. By choosing this course, they share in accepting the employers' illicit hiring of illegal immigrants. The lax Portuguese policy concerning importation of legal labour immigrants from the former African colonies, and the lack of control and prevention of the use of illegal immigrants on the Portuguese labour market, counteract the idea of creating one, large common market with free movement of capital, goods and labour in the European Union.

Germany has imported labour for decades. Since the early 1970s, the importation of labour from lands outside the EEC, later the EU, has stopped but, despite unemployment in the country, importation of labour has continued, partly from several East European countries and partly from other countries in the EU. Some of these workers are employed under atypical conditions, opening the possibility for exploitation through low pay and unsafe working conditions. By allowing, for example, English workers to be registered as self-employed, German employers are not obliged to pay social insurance contributions, as it is up to the workers themselves to pay them. If the workers fail to make these payments, they can work for German employers at lower rates of pay than German workers, who are thus subject to unfair competition. Importation of labour from Eastern Europe occurs through the use of labour permits for a restricted period, opening possibilities for under-payment in various ways. In addition to these developments in atypical forms of employment, there are also a significant number of illegal immigrants on the German labour market.

Collaboration between the trade union movement and employers' organisations is not sufficiently developed to be able to counteract the existence of large numbers of illegal immigrants on the German market, and the presence of many illegal workers demonstrates that State control is inadequate. Particularly in the building and installation sector, these conditions have created unfair competition in relation to the Danish building and installation companies who have sought work in Germany. The lax German policy in this area, too, counteracts the idea of creating one, large common market with free movement of capital, goods and labour in the European Union.

In Denmark there are practically no illegal immigrants in the labour market. The demand for the type of work that illegal immigrants can supply is limited because they lack the qualifications needed on the informal labour market. The close collaboration between the organisations concerned, both employees and employers, hinders employers from hiring illegal immigrants. There is thus no great need for State control in the workplace to uncover the employment of illegal immigrants. Denmark should demand that Germany, Portugal and the other EU countries who have many illegal immigrants on their labour markets should tighten up their policies to restrict the employment of illegal immigrants, so that the illegal and unfair competition against Danish goods and labour can be brought to a halt.

The main conclusion is that the theory that it is hardly possible for democratic countries to avoid illegal immigrants in the labour market, if they are to continue as democratic countries, is not correct. The Nordic countries are democratic. In contrast to other countries, they have a highly developed democratic collaboration between employees and employers whereby employers, through collective bargaining, undertake not to employ illegal immigrants and abide by this commitment.

Another main conclusion is that the theory that restructuring of the global economy will result in reshaping of the former industrial centres into international centres for business services, the so-called global cities, with an extremely low-paid service sector, is not general. In the former industrial countries that have maintained a high level of social welfare, no extremely low-paid service sector has arisen. A high level of productivity is maintained which, looked at from the point of view of the economy, is especially competitive. There is thus not one path of development towards a global city but two.

Notes

1 North 1993: 222. The parallel with pollution is not totally obvious, since polluters will often be large, strong industrial interests, while the same can scarcely be said of the interests behind the exploitation of illegal immigrants. North's reference to the free-rider problem, moreover, is less valid in political questions such as immigration, because politicians act out of motives of attitude or what is the norm, unlike actors in the market who optimalise, which is where the free-rider problem arises.

2 Until the break-up of the Soviet Union, Finland practised a very restrictive immigration and refugee policy. This has now changed and Finland accepts people seeking asylum along the same lines as the other Scandinavian countries.

3 But it is probably correct. There are indications that the Dutch authorities take a more relaxed view of the question of employment of illegal immigrants. "Migration News" from February 1995, states under Dutch Amnesty: "Beginning January 1, 1995, illegal immigrants in the Netherlands who can prove that have had legal work continuously for at least six years, paying both tax and social premiums, are entitled to an official residence permit. The amnesty will continue until January 1, 1999."

4   Ramakers 1996.

5   Stalker 1994.

6   Dahlgaard 1983; Feige & McGee 1989; Isachsen & Strøm 1980, 1981; Jepsen 1994; Pedersen 1991; Schneider 1986; Lundager & Schneider 1986; Sundram 1995; Viby-Mogensen 1985a, 1985b, 1987, 1989, 1990a, 1990b, 1992; Viby-Mogensen, Kvist, Körmendi & Pedersen 1995.

7   As a mathematical expression it can be described as:
$$\text{Cost}_{legal} - \text{Cost}_{illegal} > C_{discovery} \times \text{Cost}_{penalty}.$$
The profit from illegal labour must be greater than the chances of discovery times the fine.

8   Viby-Mogensen 1994: 9; Viby-Mogensen, Kvist, Körmendi & Pedersen 1995: 10-13. The theoretical literature is summarised by Cowell (1990) and Pyle (1989).

9   Sundram 1995.

2 Trends in International Economic Development

Free movement within the EU

What part does the importation by many EU countries of both legal and illegal labour from lands outside the EU play in the development of the internal common labour market within the EU? This is a complex question which has not been the subjected to systematic research in the EU.[1] I will therefore start by considering the question theoretically and, to the extent necessary, try to include empirical data.

The main reason for establishing the European Union was to create one, large common market with free movement of capital, goods and labour.[2] In this large market there is currently great disparity in the cost of labour. In this situation, according to classic economic theory, Ricardo's law of comparative benefits[3] can be called upon. This law states that international trade is independent of the principles of the comparative cost of labour. If two countries, A and B, enter into a trade relationship where each is able to produce goods X and Y, A will sell those goods for which its relative costs are lowest and correspondingly B will sell those goods for which its own comparative costs are lowest.

In a situation with free movement of capital, goods and labour, areas with low wage costs, all things being equal, will be able to out-compete corresponding goods produced in other areas with higher wage levels. Capital will pursue the low-paid areas, hoping for a better bargain. Conversely, areas with high wage levels will attract labour from areas with lower wage levels. A shortage of labour can hereby arise in the low-paid areas which will force companies in such areas to increase pay in order to retain their labour. According to classical economic theory it can therefore be expected that differences will be ironed out by the free movement of capital, goods and labour.[4]

This theory may seem disturbing to both employees and employers in areas with a high level of wage costs. Here it can be feared that free movement will mean the loss of jobs and trade to areas where the costs of wage and working conditions are much lower. The expression "social dumping" has been used to describe the disadvantageous results which many in the highly developed areas maintain can occur in a market with large differences in pay and conditions, so that countries with a low level of social welfare become competitive because of the low contributions to the social protection of labour.[5] Thus in 1992, there was, according to Flanagan, a difference in pay and fringe benefits per hour per employee in a manufacturing company of US$ 25.94 in Germany to US$ 5.01 in Portugal.[6]

This problem has of course been the subject of research; among others, Robert Flanagan above investigated the development of pay variations in the six original countries of the EU during the period 1957-1989. He concluded that the movement of labour between countries did not rise significantly and that levels of pay in the manufacturing and building sectors, on which he concentrated his study, only evened out slightly between 1957-1989.[7] Flanagan tries to explain this by a non-financial factor, pointing out that it may be wide differences in language that restrict movement of labour.[8] Wide differences in language have not, however, hindered Turks, Moroccans and people from the former Yugoslavia travelling to Western Europe and working, so it seems reasonable to ask why language differences within the EU countries should suddenly raise impassable barriers. Flanagan has not addressed this question. Even though his assertion has not been tested, it can probably be rejected.

Erickson and Kuruvilla have criticised Flanagan for only looking at labour mobility in relation to differences in pay and fringe goods, and totally ignoring the fact that higher productivity in the high-pay areas can eliminate differences in pay and thus restrict the exodus of capital to low-pay areas.[9] Instead of making comparisons on the basis of pay differences, Erickson and Kuruvilla suggest that labour costs per unit produced should be compared, because this is the figure an employer uses to calculate possible profit and decide whether to transfer capital.[10]

Erickson and Kuruvilla conclude that in 1986 there were clear differences in labour costs per unit produced between the various EU countries, and that these differences did not significantly lessen during the 1980s. Variations in labour productivity did not eliminate differences in labour costs between countries, and as a result of this there does not seem to have been any motivation for the mobility of capital in the EU as a result of labour costs. They also found that in the same period there were no significant changes in the flow of investments, and one can therefore wonder why the market has not been affected by the large differences in labour costs per unit produced, such that the wide variations still exist.

Erickson and Kuruvilla make five suggestions to explain the lack of mobility. They point out 1) that the last barriers to the free movement of capital were not removed until the beginning of 1995, 2) that there has been and still is uncertainty as to what the "Social Charter" will mean, 3) that employers in high-pay areas want highly trained labour and highly developed production systems, 4) that there are opportunities outside the EU for even lower pay costs, and 5) that low-pay areas within the EU are not sufficiently developed for the owners of capital to risk moving there.[11] They do not exclude the possibility that capital may begin to move now that all barriers to movement have been removed and goods can move freely, and that this mobility may be strengthened when final clarification of the "Social Charter" is reached and when support from the EU structure fund develops the infrastructure in the low-pay areas somewhat more. Erickson and Kuruvilla cannot therefore deny at the present time that the classic theory of the free movement of capital, goods and labour will be shown to be valid as barriers are gradually broken down.

Neither Flanagan nor Erickson and Kuruvilla address the question of whether the levelling process could be affected by the possibility, for instance, of importing cheap labour from poor countries outside the EU to areas within the EU. If the possibility exists for extremely cheap labour to flow into a local region in sufficient quantities for an unsatisfied demand for labour not arising, it must be expected that, other things being equal, the existing level of pay will be maintained or possibly fall if more labour is imported than is needed. The area will thus continue to be a low-pay area. Capital will flow in since, due to the low pay costs, goods can be produced cheaper than in high-pay areas. In this way it will be possible to out-compete production in high-pay areas or force high-pay areas to reduce their levels of pay in order to make them competitive.

Under the present conditions in the EU, it is only subjects of individual member states who can move freely to all parts of the EU and take work. If a way is opened in a low-pay area for the influx of legal and illegal immigrants to the national labour market, this can contribute to an increase in possible emigration of the country's own workers towards existing high-pay areas. It is theoretically possible to replace a part of the country's workforce with immigrants from outside the EU for a time, or even permanently.[12]

To the extent that the immigrant workforce carries out work "that would not otherwise have been performed", this workforce will, conversely, slow down development and take up resources better employed elsewhere. In this situation, the additional workforce will not attract foreign capital or lead to an increase in the sale of goods but, on the contrary, maintain the status quo. The economic effect will be similar to that of a national subsidy for the maintenance of obsolete production. It might be said that importation of cheap labour can prolong the sunset for companies on their way into the darkness.

The international movement of capital

As long as only broad concepts such as "labour", "pay", "labour costs per unit produced", "capital" and "goods" are used, the theoretical picture is quite simple. In the cases of Flanagan, and Erickson and Kuruvilla, the resultant theoretical picture does not match reality, and it is necessary to search for specific historical conditions to explain why reality does not correspond to theory. If these specific historical factors are not built into the theory and their validity is not tested, the reader is left in a state of uncertainty, as with the two examples mentioned. It is thus necessary to extend the theory to include the historical dimension, so that historical factors considered relevant can be included in it and subjected to verification.

The historical factor interesting in this connection is the development in the international division of labour. It is well known that restructuring of the global economy is currently taking place. Shortly after the Second World War, American export of capital led to an economic upswing in Western Europe and Japan from the end of the 1950s to the end of the 1960s. Despite the exodus from agriculture and the mobilisation of housewives, a growing demand for labour in industry and the service sector arose during this period, especially in the northern and central parts of Western Europe, which resulted in pressure on wages.[13] This partly triggered an import of foreign labour and partly an export of capital to areas that could offer low levels of pay. The massive export of capital from the USA, Japan and Western

Europe to South-east and Southern Asia and to parts of South America in the late 1960s and early 1970s led to the foundation of a number of new centres of growth, at the same time as the former industrial centres experienced a decline. Some of the former centres are today net importers of industrial goods produced as a result of their own export of capital, and some are now experiencing a de-industrialisation process.

This restructuring of the global economy and the recession in the former industrial centres worries many people. They believe a permanent fall in the number of jobs will occur, which will particularly affect the weakest segments of the labour force (unskilled men and especially women, coloureds and immigrants) in the former centres, and result in permanent mass unemployment. This may be too pessimistic a view, resulting from the researchers concerned building on too narrow an understanding of the international movement of capital and its effects. The movement of capital, according to Sassen-Koob,[14] should not be seen as a one-way process that is complete as soon as it is carried out. She believes that when one of the former industrial centres experiences a serious economic recession as a result of manufacturing industries moving to one of the new industrial centres, potential conditions for profitable investments in the old centre must theoretically be re-established, she believes. This presupposes that the former industrial centre contains resources that can be considered as useful to capital. These resources can, for instance, be that the former industrial centre has a highly developed infrastructure and public service system, a well-trained workforce which has lost its political power because the manufacturing companies have closed and many are unemployed, and that there is a local government eager to attract investments. According to Sassen-Koob, all this forms a kind of reservoir of unused utility value, which, in certain circumstances, can be utilised by capital to make profits.

Global cities

As manufacturing companies disappear from the former industrial centres, a number of new economic activities can arise there. According to Sassen-Koob, these are highly specialised forms of business services. In the USA there has been a geographical scattering of manufacturing companies because of new investment in less-developed areas. This development has not only created changes in the way in which production is organised but has also created a need for new types of production and the need to ensure management, control and development for this new organisation of production. The development of management, control and planning contributions is, according to Sassen-Koob, mainly concentrated in the large urban areas in the former industrial centres, which she calls "global cities". These have become centres for the production of highly developed service products such as expertise in legal matters, management, communication, financial matters, technical skills, engineering ability, accounting, marketing, consultancy help and many other forms of service products.

On the basis of her analysis, which was concentrated on New York and Los Angeles, she claims that the development of these advanced service products is the fastest growing sector in the US economy, seen in relation to its share of national product, employment as an export. The development in the pattern of employment and social structure points towards growth in high-income jobs where educational requirements are high, and in low-income jobs, where qualification requirements are modest, while traditional middle-income jobs will decrease.

Her demonstration of the growth in low-income jobs in the service sector is her most surprising and important discovery. It departs from the gloomy visions that restructuring of the global economy and the industrial recession in the former industrial centres will provoke a permanent fall in the number of jobs for the weakest segments of the workforce (women, coloured and immigrants). Sassen-Koob claims that the reverse is true. Developments in different income categories in the service industry from 1950 to 1975 show an increase of 35% in the number of jobs in the two highest income-groups, of 11.3% in the medium income-groups, and of 54% in the number of jobs for the lowest income-groups. Sassen-Koob believes that this is why immigrants and ethnic minorities move into the larger cities in great numbers. They have better opportunities to get jobs there, even if at lower pay.

Cohen has pointed out this "global city" hypothesis requires a more empirical foundation before it can seriously be considered valid.[15] "Global cities" are metropolises where the professional and management classes meet, where hotel chains such as Intercontinental, Sheraton and Hilton are established, where there are frequent international air connections, and with stock exchanges, theatres, sophisticated entertainment, and international educational and research institutions. As far as growth in low income jobs is concerned, they are connected with a wide range of service tasks, e.g.

cleaning, shop assistants, transport, serving, prostitution and other forms of entertainment.

Looking at the trends in the development of a large European city like Copenhagen, there are many indications that this metropolis is on its way to qualifying under Sassen-Koob's definition of a "global city". There has been a clear fall in the number of jobs in the industrial sector at the same time as the service sector has become more and more dominant. There has especially been a clear and distinct growth in business services, and Copenhagen is today an international business service centre with an international airport, and a number of international hotel chains such as Sheraton and Intercontinental. However, on one point there is a clear discrepancy. This is the development of a large, extremely low-paid consumer service. In contrast to the USA, no rapid growth in the number of extremely low paid-jobs has occurred, despite the fact that there has been significant unemployment in the last two decades. This raises the question why a marginalisation process has not arisen to create a number of extremely low paid jobs in the consumer service branch in Denmark. Why does a phenomenon such as "the working poor" not exist in Denmark, despite the fact that Denmark has had considerable unemployment for many years?

The post-industrial society

Sassen-Koob's hypothesis on the restructuring of capitalism contains no precise theoretical explanation of the processes that force one particular group down into the low paid jobs in the big, new service sector. She talks about the workforce having lost its political power as a result of a decline in employment in the industrial sector. Many are forced out of necessity to accept employment at extremely low rates of pay in the service sector. Why does this occur in the USA and England? Why has there not been a strengthening of the trade union organisations, which could stem this development instead? Considerations such as these do not enter into her deliberations. Market forces alone control development as a natural law. It is necessary to look more closely at these conditions and to devise a theoretical explanation as to why certain countries, such as the USA, experience a marginalisation and impoverishment of employees in the new service sector, while other countries, such as Denmark, have not created a phenomenon like "the working poor".

A search in the recent literature about "class" and "social stratification" leads one into a supermarket with numerous offers of hypotheses and theories. The question of the formation of social classes or, as some express it nowadays, "social stratification in post-industrial society"[16] has absorbed many researchers. Libraries bulge with hypotheses and theories about class formation in the post-industrial society. It is an ideological battle-field, with widely diverging opinions depending on whether one seeks inspiration from the old masters such as Marx and Weber, from the new theoreticians such as Bordieu and Giddens, or whether one totally rejects these and doubts whether it is at all possible, on the basis of inherited concepts and class theories, to understand the question of developments in the new employment structures in the former industrial centres, with their life chances and inequalities.

It was impractical to take everything down from the shelves for closer inspection, but for non-Marxist sociologists the concept of class is nowadays considered to be blanketed in an atmosphere of total decay. It was created, it is said, at a time and under social conditions, which no longer reflect the reality of the present day, and is therefore no longer suitable as an analytical instrument. To this group of researchers belongs Daniel Bell, one of the theoreticians behind the concept of "the post-industrial society".[17]

Bell believes that, from an historical viewpoint, the notion of a class-divided society became obsolete with the development of welfare capitalism and the appearance of the new middle classes. In step with the movement towards the post-industrial society, the class-divided society disappeared. Post-industrial society is characterised by employment in the service sector becoming dominant. Groups of highly-trained technocrats will appear, who will reach a privileged position through their control of knowledge and modern methods of communication. They will form a meritocracy, where merits in the form of higher education will become a key criterion for assignment and a share of the privileges. In this way, a society will appear with fundamentally different requirements, where the deep class divisions of the past, founded on proprietary ownership rights to production factors, will be eroded. Bell is blind to the possibility that a new underclass may emerge.

In his critique of Marx, Bell makes the mistake of believing that production's social relationships follow the technical production conditions that define the degree of technological development. It is misleading to claim that technological developments abolish capitalism. Society has developed technologically; machines have arrived and new methods of organising work have appeared that can increase the productivity of the workforce, but this has not altered the dominant conditions for production, which are capitalist. Bell is guilty of confusing different analytical planes. Similar visions with minor variations have been presented by numbers of other authors.[18]

The latest example of the confusion of analytical planes in the treatment of the problem of class is presented in the book "Changing Classes", published by an international research group led by the Danish sociologist Gøsta Esping-Andersen, a professor at the European University in Florence. Esping-Andersen postulates that the traditional concept of class has lost its analytical value as we find ourselves in a world characterised by post-industrial employment, i.e. employment in the production of service contributions.[19]

After a short description of a number of the newer theoretical analyses of the concept of class, Esping-Andersen rejects all those based on Marx, Weber and Durkheim as worthless, without having subjected them to any form of critical analysis. He simply asserts that the old formations of the concept of class are not applicable in an analysis of conditions in present-day post-industrial society. This, he asserts, is because the classic concept of class developed by Marx and Weber among others was formed at a time when social institutions were totally different from nowadays. Mass education, the welfare state and collective bargaining were institutions totally unknown to Marx, Weber and Durkheim, and it is these new institutional creations that have generated completely different prerequisites for class formation than those existing at the time when the traditional classic concepts were developed. Therefore they can no longer be applied. If they are used, he maintains, important new lines in the development of social inequality in modern society may be overlooked, so it is necessary to es-tablish new concepts and theories.

From a scientific point of view, this is not a serious way to reason. It would seem that Esping-Andersen fails to understand what Marx's and Weber's concept of class represents. Seen from a Marxist point of view, Esping-Andersen confuses two different analytical planes in the same way as Bell does. What he is talking about is technological development, where we have mass education, the welfare state and collective bargaining, but this has not in any way altered the dominant social relationships, which are still capitalist production conditions. Nor does he give any precise definition of the concept of class, or of social structure and social change. He asserts that,

"Traditional class theory tends to be institution-less, assuming that classes emerge out of unfettered exchange relations, be it in the market or at the 'point of production'."[20]

He asserts that in the modern post-industrial society, class formation has many roots and that it is important analytically to distinguish between a "fordist" division of labour and a "post-fordist" division of labour.[21] By the term "fordist" he understands standardised mass-production coupled to mass-consumption, while "post-fordist" does not in the same way describe a standardised mass-production corresponding precisely to that found in an industrial concern. About this he says:

"Reconsider the McDonald's fast-food counter workers. Their jobs may be highly taylorized, but they nonetheless have to possess social skills that, in a factory, are quite irrelevant: an engaging smile, courtesy, youthful enthusiasm. For career promotion into, say, McDonald's management, these kinds of social skills are very likely to be determinant."[22]

He also states:

"McDonald's and Burger King outlets represent probably the most advanced type of taylorism and mass standardization in the consumer services. But since customers seek personal services precisely because they are personal and cater to individual demands and tastes, the potential for massive fordization should be modest indeed."[23]

Esping-Andersen lacks precision in his concept formations, but in the book "Changing Classes", a number of empirical stratification and mobility analyses are carried out on a variety of societies. These, according to Esping-Andersen, show that a distinct post-industrial class structure is being established. In the post-industrial society there will be unattractive jobs. The majority of people taking these unattractive jobs are not condemned to lifetime servitude, as used to be the case. Therefore, claims Esping-Andersen, the pessimists are mistaken when they see the future as a mass-proletarianisation of service workers.

Esping-Andersen claims that the new unskilled workers in the service sector, in contrast to unskilled workers in industry, are not as structurally locked fast. The new service industries occupy people who are willing, for a period, to undertake an unpleasant job in the service sector.

"They are structurally quite undetermined, fluid particles on the way to something else, be it careers, unemployment or mothering. They are not a class, but people temporarily willing or forced to take unpleasant jobs."[24]

Education becomes the main determinant of an individual's chances in life. This can, according to Esping-Andersen, give rise to great clefts. In Germany, the education factor raises huge barriers against social mobility; in other countries conditions are different. The formation of social layers in the post-industrial society will therefore depend on education. In this connection it is pointed out that social qualifications can play a crucial role in the chances of mobility, and that these social qualifications will, to a high degree, be determined by the environment in which one grows up. According to Esping-Andersen, the post-industrial labour market will be characterised by jobs for women, but it is possible that in the long run women will be out-competed by men and forced back into the home. The competition for work is expected to lead to a downward pressure on wages, so that they will fall.

Furthermore, Esping-Andersen believes that if only universal access to education is ensured by society, even people in low-paid jobs and their children will be able to attain the social mobility to counteract the formation of social divides. As to how he visualises this in concrete terms, he gives no hint. This should not be surprising, for it has as yet been impossible to find a method of securing educational opportunities which will ensure everyone an equal chance of an education.[25]

The significance of surplus labour

As a third example of a more recent analysis of the concept of class, I have chosen Anthony Giddens' work from the beginning of the 1970s (*The Class Structure of the Advanced Societies*). Here is a researcher who by means of a serious scientific method sets as his objective the performance of a re-evaluation of the concept of class, based on the works of Marx and Weber, as he believes many researchers' "disillusionment with the concept of class to be one which rests on false premises".[26] He begins by saying:

"When, however, I began a systematic analysis of the literature of fairly recent origin upon the theory of class structure, I was struck by its very sparseness - not in terms of its numerical strength but in terms of its analytical penetration. Confusion and ambiguity in the use of the term 'class' are abundantly evident; but distinctive and considered attempts to revise the theory of class upon a broad scale are few indeed."[27]

Giddens seriously and critically attempts to analyse the various formulations of concepts, but despite his talent and systematic, he is too hasty and his attempt therefore lacks sufficient analytical depth. Where he takes the easy way out is when he comes to Marx's labour theory of value. This states that only labour that can supply a product with surplus value is productive work and that the purpose of the capitalist in investing and getting workers started on production is to create surplus value.[28] The classic conflict of interest between capital and labour thus, in Giddens' interpretation, comprises the capitalist class on the one hand and on the other the working class, where the latter only consists of workers who perform productive work, i.e. workers who carry out the actual production of commodities. He therefore concludes that workers who are not engaged in productive work, i.e. who do not produce surplus value, hold a shadowy, ambiguous position in Marxist theory.[29] Therefore there is a need for a new theory.

Here Giddens is mistaken. By focusing exclusively on surplus value, he fails to notice that the source of surplus value is surplus labour. When the worker, by selling his labour to the capitalist, takes his place in the production of commodities, he receives a wage. As Qvortrup has shown, the labour for which the capitalist pays is worth more than the wages paid, since through productive work it produces a value which in part covers the capitalist's costs in the form of the worker's pay, and in part forms a surplus value, created by the worker contributing surplus labour for which he is not paid.

By means of a thorough analysis of the works of Marx, especially the later publications, Qvortrup has convincingly demonstrated, that it is not primarily the distinction between productive and unproductive labour that is the basis of class division, but rather whether the work contains surplus labour.[30]

In his analysis, Qvortrup focuses on one of Marx's two classic concepts, namely the *an-sich* concept of class.[31] Like many others, Giddens focuses on the phenomenon that capital appropriates the surplus value of the labour force it employs in the sphere of production, and he is also well aware that in the sphere of circulation, according to Marx, surplus value cannot be created, and that work thus performed as unproductive work in the Marxist sense does not add value to the product.[32] However, the capitalist concentrates on appropriating surplus value but, in order to have a share in it, the capitalist must in certain situations employ workers who do not, through their labour, produce surplus value. The capitalist is not primarily interested in knowing who creates the surplus value, but in getting hold of it. The capitalist purchases a temporary disposition over a person's labour; this labour contains more value than the wages he pays, since it contains surplus labour. Seen from a capitalist's viewpoint, the only employee who is of value is one who performs surplus labour and who can either directly or indirectly give him a share in the surplus value.

Thus what the individual employees in a capitalist concern do is irrelevant, as long as they perform surplus labour for their employer in relation to their pay, which ensures that he obtains a share in the surplus value that is created somewhere in the system. Qvortrup can thus conclude:

> "Whether the work is machine work or office work, if it is well paid or badly, manual or intellectual is not crucial, only abstract work in general, measured in the expended hours of work - its value - can be the starting-point for a definition of this work."[33]

In Qvortrup's interpretation of Marx's *an-sich* concept of class (class in itself), there is not, as Giddens asserts *anything shadowy or ambiguous* in it. Everyone employed for a wage by a capitalist investor belongs, when looked at objectively, to the working class, i.e. the *an-sich* concept of class (class for itself), and this obviously also includes wage-earners employed in trade and service and, in the latter case, in the private and public sectors. Whether these wage-earners are conscious of their situation politically is a matter concerning the *für-sich* concept of class.

The dual labour market

It is well known that developments in capitalist production methods have, over the course of time, resulted in a number of extensive polarisation processes within the working class. Companies have grown. This has created a fast-growing staff of administrative and office workers.[34] A growth in the production of commodities has occurred which has led to a growth in the number of jobs in commerce, transport and other forms of service. The functions of the state have grown both in number and extent, and have created numerous jobs in the public service sector where employees, in parity with employees in the private, capitalist manufacturing sector, are subject to the employer's requirements as to productivity and efficiency.

Even though mass education, the welfare state and collective bargaining did not exist in Marx's time, these developments can in my opinion, still be analysed meaningfully using the conceptual apparatus that Marx devised. The social organisation of production, for instance the capitalist production mode, has not disappeared as a result of technological production conditions having evolved, so that we now have mass education, a welfare state and collective bargaining. Marx's conceptual apparatus comprises scientific abstract models that can be used to illuminate empirical reality, including amongst other things the technological development of modern capitalism.

To explain the developments that have taken place within the framework of the capitalist production mode, Doeringer and Piore's hypothesis on the dual labour market[35] can be applied. This asserts that competition and the ever-growing requirements for productivity and efficiency to which by and large all work places are subject creates a division of employees into an A team and a B team. Looking at the company level, there have arisen, as Schierup mentions[36] "internal labour markets" in many strong and successful companies. As he says, referring to Boje[37] and Åberg,[38]

"These are companies which invest in an organisational structure characterised by teamwork, the spirit of co-operation, high motivation in the individual employee and intensive exchange of knowledge. Here the taylorist principle that labour must be rigidly subordinated to the production process is abandoned in preference for a perspective where employees are regarded as a *creative resource*. Under these conditions, a rational business strategy contains a kind of selection where competence is regarded as unique and as an investment for the concern. Appointment to a position no longer occurs through an open market characterised by its competitiveness, but through considerate training, upgrading and mobility within a concern. If new employees are appointed, it is after careful selection."

Management positions are often filled via consultancy bureaux, applicants often having to pass through various selection procedures where not only professionalism is studied, but also factors such as loyalty, etc. Less important positions are often filled on the basis of personal recommendation, both for office staff and hourly-paid workers.

"Companies require unconditional loyalty and personal engagement on the part of their *members of staff.* In return, they offer employees fair working conditions, job security, and good opportunities for training and a career within the framework of the company's internal labour market."[39]

This results in the creation of the A team, but at the same time other workers are employed to carry out jobs which are routine, uninteresting, unhealthy, less qualified and connected with temporary and insecure working conditions. These are on the B team. This type of job is separated organisationally from the concern's more privileged internal labour market. This causes an even sharper divide between the company's career-minded personnel and the workers performing routine tasks.

Another strategy is to allocate less attractive work to subcontractors, so that recessions hit their employees first.

Thus in many successful companies a growing difference is developed between working conditions for the A team and the B team. For the individual, it is important to get onto the A team in order to avoid the recession-sensitive, insecure working conditions on the B team. The abolition of many middle-management positions has made it difficult to get onto the A team, where more and more weight is laid on teamwork that is responsible for a complicated and expensive production apparatus.[40] New demands are made. These involve greater requirements for personal flexibility, but also a growing demand for linguistic communication. Significant economic responsibility is laid directly on the individual work-groups, who gain extensive influence in the planning and internal allocation of their own work, as well as in recruitment of new colleagues. In many cases pay is made directly dependent on the results of the individual work-group to a degree that was impossible within the framework of earlier forms of labour organisation, or with the collective consciousness and the collective trade union strategies that previously dominated working life.

In line with company management strategies, employees themselves aim today at recruiting people with the necessary competence to complete the groups internal division of labour. At the same time, irrespective of individuals' technical and formal professional competence, purely personal relationships within the single work-group are becoming more and more important. Autonomous work-groups try to avoid anything that can appear unexpectedly; possible socially disturbing elements in the group's communication and co-operation, which may potentially delay the flow of work, reduce results and diminish pay. One becomes extremely selective when it comes to recruiting new people into the group. In contrast to the broad solidarity characteristic of many classic labour collectives, result-oriented competition between smaller work-groups creates a spirit of *us against all the rest*. One therefore gambles among other things on recruiting through a personal network. They want people in whom they already know, or "friends of friends". The group becomes a closed, socially homogenous unit, trying to keep "strangers" out. To the extent that this strategy cannot supply a sufficient workforce, consultancy firms are employed to "head hunt", where weight is not only laid on finding people with the right professional qualifications but where social qualifications are also given high priority.

Within the framework of modern internal labour markets, we see on the one hand the development of a heterogeneous structure in groups, when it concerns individual professional qualifications that are an internal division of labour within the group between various individuals who combine a general education with the necessary individual specialised knowledge. On the other hand, the work-groups become more and more homogenous in social composition.[41]

As mentioned above, polarisation takes place in and between all work places. Polarisation of labour has occurred in what may be called the planning, controlling and administrative functions, which set high demands on the labour-force's professional qualifications in the form of education. On the other hand there still exists a taylorisation of labour functions that sets lower and lower demands on the labour-force's educational qualifications. People with differing goals in life are in demand at the opposite ends of the scale.

The past influencing the present

One problem connected with the many attempts to devise new theories on social stratification is that insufficient regard is paid to the fact that the present, so-called post-industrial epoch is shaped to a great extent by the influence of history. The people who constitute the present were born in the past. They were born into different environments, which influenced them during childhood and adolescence. Through parents, siblings and other close friends and relatives, each individual is brought up to understand the difference between right and wrong in his particular environment and what is considered the correct way of life. Through socialisation, the individual imperceptibly learns to perceive his way of life, or the ideal he strives after, as natural and proper. This will influence his consciousness and way of thinking. The individual regards what he experiences as the "objective" truth, and not as something formed by his own conception of the world - his ideology. Ideology is invisible but is, despite this, a powerful force in the lifestyle of human beings. All are bound by specific lifestyles independent of their own will. What people want is determined by their culture.

If the conditions of existence for a particular lifestyle disappear, its followers will seek alternative conditions that make it possible for them to continue their way of life. If these do not exist, the lifestyle will die out.

The polarisation described by Doeringer and Piore forms the basis for development in two specific cultures. One is what Højrup has called the careerist lifestyle, and the other is the wage-earner's lifestyle. In his search for profit, the capitalist thus creates living conditions for two types of social institutions in the working classes.[42]

In the careerist lifestyle, work plays the dominant role, typically tied to the organisational, developmental and controlling work processes. The character of the work, together with the company's and organisation's hierarchical structure, forms its basis. The workforce's educational background is the foundation for a career path that is additionally determined by the degree of engagement in one's work and the pursuit of personal and career development leading to further qualifications. Work is of central significance to the way of life, as reproduction is closely connected to the course of a career. Existence outside work is organised, as far as possible for the benefit of the career, so the careerist lifestyle experiences less contrast between work and leisure.

The careerist lifestyle is typically a white-collar one. Life is shaped by the career, and this can demand geographical as well as social mobility. The purpose of work, according to people with this lifestyle, is to make a career. The purpose of working life, and for that matter also leisure and family life, is to achieve increasingly higher positions with ever-increasing authority. It is purely the personal and individual future goal that is the motive power.

Figure 1: Model of social formation

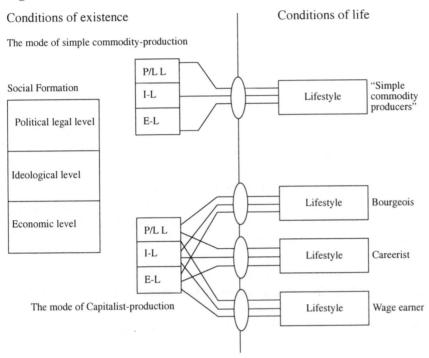

Source: Jan Hjarnø, Danish Centre for Migration and Ethnic Studies.

A good starting point for a decent career is a high level of education. However, as Højrup says, long education is not always enough.

"A prerequisite for promotion is that one makes a major contribution to one's work. It must literally engross the particular individual and, in order to take part in the competition for promotion, normal working hours are not always sufficient. In other words, family life must also provide the possibilities for investment in the career. This can be through the use of leisure periods for courses and further education. It can also take place through the family moving in the right circles where contacts valuable to the career are made and maintained. It can happen in lodges, through social life, through participation in certain exclusive sports, etc. In connection with all these, it is necessary for the family, by their manners, taste, clothing, house, car, cookery and leisure to demonstrate that they belong to and can be accepted by the particular circles. The whole of this symbolic world ensures that one says 'How do you do' to the *right people* and that people *do not get each other wrong.*"[43]

In the careerist lifestyle, family life does not play an insignificant role in working life, but the effects work both ways. The family's way of behaving is important to the careerist's course of promotion, but conversely the family's status and consumer possibilities are dependent on the career.

In the wage-earner's lifestyle, which is especially tied to manual work in manufacturing and the service industry, work is regarded as necessity for obtaining the economic means needed to be able to take part in the leisure activities thought to give meaning to life. This can be owning and looking after an allotment, a country cottage, holidays in Majorca, etc. As regards content, the wage-earner's lifestyle is characterised by having little influence over his employment. Work is something given by others. It is activities outside work that give meaning to life. One works to make it possible to live. In the wage-earner's lifestyle, there is normally a sharp differentiation between work and leisure. Leisure is the goal. One works to earn leisure.

In the wage-earner's lifestyle, the family has no solidarity around work. The family has a home where its members sleep, eat, take care of hygiene, wash their clothes, relax, experience their intimate life and keep their private property. Ideologically, the home is regarded as the point of departure for daily activities. The various family members have different functions. Normally the wife is responsible for shopping, cooking and cleaning. Even though sexual roles are becoming less rigid, it is still common for the wife to function as the "service centre" for the rest of the family. In cases where spouses cannot agree, marriages dissolve and a family form arises consisting of a single adult with children.

In addition to the two lifestyles described, there is a third one in the capitalist scheme of things, namely the bourgeois lifestyle practised by the investor.[44]

The lifestyles described above are the result of a long historical developmental process.[45] People bear these lifestyles and they affect their actions in the present. Therefore it is correct to say that the past influences the present.

The simple commodity production mode

Through a study of direct production, Højrup found a strategy other than the capitalist one for the organisation of production, linked to which was a special lifestyle, which he called the "self-employed lifestyle". As an Althusserian, he speaks of the so-called "simple commodity mode of production",[46] but this is about a strategy which is not exclusively tied to direct production, since it also occurs in commerce and service in the private sector.

Instead of designating it as the simple commodity mode of production, we ought rather to use the designation "the simple commodity and service mode of production". This simple commodity and service mode of production can be defined by its producers (understood here as the working people) themselves owning the means of production.[47] They are often specialised. Fishermen produce fish, farmers corn, meat and other agricultural produce, etc. These are things or services that have a utility use for other people. Through selling them, they obtain purchasing power to buy things and services they need but which they do not produce themselves. By being traded, the products and services become commodities, and the production is thus commodity production.

According to classic economic theory, production in a liberal society is controlled by market competition. All products have an exchange value, which corresponds to the expenditure incurred in obtaining raw materials, maintaining the means of production, and paying the workforce. If the producers are unable to attain a price on the market, which corresponds to their commodities' exchange value, they must stop production. This automatic process regulates the division of labour in society and is called *the law of value*.

The law of value assumes that producers always utilise their production capacity to the full, so they are unable to react to a fall in market prices by increasing production. The law also assumes that there is a fixed lower limit for the value required for the reproduction of the workforce.

These assumptions are not always valid when dealing with the simple commodity production mode. Here people are "only" producing in order to maintain their lifestyle as self-employed, and production capacity far from always fully utilised. We see this in Danish agriculture, where farmers make full use of their production capacity at certain periods, while at others, when their debts are lower, they cut down production to a level which gives them sufficient returns to maintain their former lifestyle. In periods with falling prices, one can however experience some farmers "reacting" by increasing production through utilising their reserve capacity. There is suddenly room for a few more pigs in each sty, etc.

According to Højrup, the simple commodity producer will prefer to increase production in order to survive rather than halting it when market prices fall in relation to the exchange value. This is where a significant difference lies compared with the capitalist production mode, where the attempt is made to utilise capacity optimally in order to obtain the largest possible return, and where capital is withdrawn if the yield is too low in comparison with other investment possibilities.

The assumption of the law of value, that a fixed lower limit exists for the cost of labour, does not necessarily apply when considering simple commodity producers. In the simple commodity production mode, the producer himself owns all the necessary production factors, including his own labour. He produces in order to maintain his lifestyle as simple commodity producer or, in other words, as self-employed, and does not stop production even though earnings fall. He tries to survive the fall by reducing expenditure or obtaining supplementary income by starting a subsidiary occupation, while hoping that earning opportunities will improve. This course of action has been very typical of Danish family farmers (smallholders). When it is impossible to make ends meet for a while, either the man or the wife has taken employment outside the family concern. As far as simple commodity producers are concerned, the law of value is only significant in relation to how many producers there is room for to supply to the market.

The market mechanism requires that for every commodity a price is set which tends to be equal to the commodity's exchange value. If a producer introduces a new production technology so that he can produce more goods in the same time, he will reduce the exchange value of his goods. As long as the old exchange value decides the market price, he will make a profit equivalent to the difference between the exchange value of his goods and the market price. He can reduce his market price and therefore out-compete other producers. This will force the others to introduce new technology, and this competition will ensure a technologically equal level appearing in society.

The simple commodity producer must turn out products and services at a level at which they will have exchange value for others. This normally means that the producer must carry out a long manufacturing process in his own concern, and this again requires the producer to have the necessary professional skills himself. The producer must himself organise and control his production and take responsibility for the work being carried out well enough for the commodity or service to be of quality which will enable it to be sold. The producer also has the personal responsibility for ensuring that the commodities produced do not cost so much that they cannot earn the profits necessary for the concern to continue. Finally he is also responsible for investing in technology to be able to compete with other producers.

This situation creates special circumstances for the simple commodity producer's lifestyle. However, it is not usually an individual person, but of some form of collaborating group, who own and run a production unit in co-operation. In Danish agriculture, the family farm is the normal production unit, with the family as the collaborating group. In Copenhagen, for instance, families of Pakistani origins have established cleaning companies. The collaborating group can, however, have other forms and it is not possible to deduce from the production mode concept itself how these collaborating groups are structured and recruited.

The self-employed lifestyle

The production mode concept only determines through production conditions and work-process structures which social framework is set for the collaborating group's work. In order to clarify the form of the collaborating group it is necessary to look at cultural structures in society, i.e. lifestyles as they manifest themselves in reality.

The simple commodity production mode determines a type of lifestyle which Højrup has called "the self-employed lifestyle".[48] Simple commodity producers have a lifestyle by which the producers themselves carry out the manufacture of products to a level at which they have exchange value for others. In each production unit, the producer must carry out the complete manufacturing process himself. The producer must himself possess the craftsmanship and other qualities necessary, and organise and control the course of the work himself. It is the producer who is responsible for the work being carried out properly, so that the commodity or service attains a quality that makes it possible for it to be sold in competition with other producers' goods and services. The simple commodity producer is also personally responsible for the goods or services produced not costing so much that they cannot earn the profit necessary for the concern to continue.

Large numbers of paid workers are not usually employed in the simple commodity producer's production unit. There is often no exploitation between the workers and the employer. The producer owns the company himself and possesses the qualifications necessary to carry out production. The concern is the foundation of the producer's entire existence, and it is therefore vitally important for him to preserve it.

During periods when a business has difficulty making a profit large enough to support the producer, one often sees either the man or his wife, if it is a family business, taking paid employment to supplement the income from their own business and to obtain the means to continue trading. Such paid employment is normally only regarded as a necessary means to procure income. It is still the "free" work at home in the concern that gives life its meaning and which it is hoped will again form the foundation of the family's existence one day.

Simple commodity producers normally make no sharp distinction between work and leisure. They blend together into a goal-oriented day's work, that this day's work is a goal in itself, carried out at one's own inner urging and experienced as meaningful. The last thing one would do as a simple commodity producer is sell one's business and give up one's existence as a self-employed tradesman in order to work, for instance, as an employee in manufacturing or some other concern. For the simple commodity producer, life only has meaning as a free and self-employed tradesman.

The effect of lifestyles

Changes in the employment situation can affect the conditions of existence for the bearers of the various lifestyles. Because they vary, their view of the situation and their reactions to it will vary, and what this can lead to has been the subject of research to only a slightly lesser extent. Individuals with different lifestyles can thus be expected to react differently to unemployment, but before discussing and analysing this set of problems it is necessary to look more closely at the phenomenon of unemployment itself.

Notes

1 In January 1996, Ramakers presented a survey of research concerning illegal immigrants. The majority of research focused on developments within individual countries and has seldom interconnected different types of migration, e.g. legal immigration, illegal immigration, brain gain, etc. The most popular analysis model has been a push-pull model under which migration is looked at from an individualistic point of view. Individualistic factors influence migration; individuals migrate for many different reasons: the desire to avoid oppression or starvation, economic ambition, reunion of families, education, etc. It has been common that, through questionnaire investigations, a list of such "push" and "pull" factors has been put together and presented as a migration theory. Through questionnaire investigations of this type, the percentage for each reason can be confirmed, which can be useful as a first demarcation to the question: "Who migrates"? However, these studies cannot explain the structural factors which decide migration patterns in time, space and extent (Ramakers 1996).

2 The Common European Act, art. 13, EFT.Nr.L. 169/7. "Push" and "pull" factors have been put together and presented as a migration theory. Through questionnaire investigations of this type, the percentage for each reason can be confirmed, which can be useful as a first demarcation to the question: "Who migrates"? However, these studies cannot explain the structural factors, which decide migration patterns in time, space and extent (Ramakers 1996).

3 Ricardo 1926: 77-93.

4 Despite extensive economic collaboration between the EU countries, there are great differences in the individual countries' occupational structure. The Southern European countries and Eire are characterised by a relatively large agricultural sector, with correspondingly smaller service and manufacturing sectors. In Portugal in 1989, 18.9% of the labour force were employed in agriculture, 35.3% in the manufacturing sector and 45.7% in the service sector. The corresponding figures for Denmark were 6.0% in the agricultural sector, 26.8% in the manufacturing sector and 67.3% in the service sector (Eurostat 1991).

5 Mosely 1990: 160. See also Due, Madsen & Jensen 1992: 64-47.

6   Flanagan 1993: Pay costs per hour worked in 1990, including payments to various forms of social contributions, were in Danish kroner: Germany kr. 133.80, Sweden kr. 133.80, Finland kr. 125.40, Holland kr. 117.00, Belgium kr. 117.00, Denmark kr. 108.50, Italy kr. 102.40, France kr. 97.20, Great Britain kr. 77.30, Eire kr. 72.10, Spain kr. 71.10 and Portugal kr. 21.90 (Finansredegørelse '91: 195, Copenhagen 1991).

7   Flanagan 1993.

8   Flanagan 1993: 184.

9   Erickson & Kuruvilla 1994: 29.

10 Erickson & Kuruvilla 1994: 29.

11 Erickson & Kuruvilla 1994: 45.

12 As long as high-pay areas remain so.

13 Albæk, Madsen & Pedersen have constructed a model of pay-rises and unemployment in Denmark in the period 1950-1990, which demonstrates how the fall in employment to 1-2% in the 1960s and early 1970s closely corresponds with pay rises in the same period (Albæk, Madsen & Pedersen 1992: 22).

14 Sassen-Koob 1983, 1984, 1987.

15 Cohen 1987.

16 Esping-Andersen 1993.

17 Bell: 1976.

18 Kern & Schumann 1984; Piore & Sabel 1984; Boyer 1988.

19 Esping-Andersen 1993.

20 Esping-Andersen 1993: 2.

21 Esping-Andersen's use of the term "fordism" is confusing. His explanation is: "The concept of fordism, as used by Piore and Sabel (1984) and the French Regulation School (see Boyer, 1988), refers to the epoch of standardized mass production, coupled with mass-consumption, but connotes more broadly the overall macro-arrangement of economic activity and management, including Keynesian demand management to uphold mass consumption and a relatively rigid organization of the production process with its hierarchy of management-worker relations. Our use of the concept denotes primarily the stratification aspects of fordism, in particular the phenomenon of the standard mass-production worker".

22 Esping-Andersen 1993: 31.

23 Esping-Andersen 1993: 31.
24 Esping-Andersen 1993: 239.
25 Glasser 1972; Hjarnø 1996.
26 Giddens 1973: 10.
27 Giddens 1973: 10.
28 "In capitalism, labour is treated on a par with any other commodity, as a product to be bought and sold on the market. But what the worker sells, in fact, is his labour-*power*, an economic capacity, which can be quantified and assessed in terms of a monetary standard in common with the material products of his labour. Surplus value is explained by reference to the fact that, as the labour-power of the worker is a commodity, its 'cost of production' can be calculated just like any other commodity. This is constituted by the cost of providing the worker with sufficient return to 'produce and reproduce himself': the differential between this and the total value created by the worker is the source of surplus value" (Giddens 1973: 34).
29 Giddens 1973: 96.
30 Qvortrup 1971: 20.
31 By the *an-sich* concept of class, is meant, according to Qvortrup: "the elements which constitute the common situation, the objective economic and social conditions which they have in common". The *für-sich* concept of class, on the other hand, refers to the situation where the members of a class have become conscious of their situation and, for instance, make conscious use of it in their political struggle (Qvortrup 1971).
32 It is hardly possible to provide a precise empirical definition of what can be classified unconditionally as productive or unproductive labour.
33 Qvortrup 1971: 19-20.
34 Geiger 1948: 41-44.
35 Doeringer & Piore 1971.
36 Schierup 1993: 112-114.
37 Boje 1991: 40ff.
38 Åberg 1989.
39 Schierup 1993: 113.
40 Hjarnø 1991.
41 Schierup 1993: 115.

42 Capitalist production methods also, of course, provide conditions for the existence of that social institution in which the capitalist lives, the bourgeois way of life. They will not be discussed further.

43 Højrup 1984: 154-155.

44 By this is meant companies in the private sector, run by owners with the primary motive of creating profits, and where the owners will be motivated to withdraw their investment if the returns on their investments sink to below an average return, preferring instead to invest in activities supplying a greater return.

45 The concept of lifestyle is a theoretical construction. In the empirical world, individuals can be characterised to a greater or lesser extent by various lifestyles. The individual person's ideology and actions can contain attributes from several lifestyles, but since there are limits to how great an inconsistency there can be in the individual's opinions and actions, one of the lifestyles will dominate. It is with this background that I mean one can speak of the bearer of a lifestyle. The lifestyle model is thus not a tool for the direct and precise classification of individuals in an empirical population, described in official statistics about active employment.

46 Wallerstein 1977: 29-49; Portes & Walton 1981.

47 For me the essence is that one owns one's workplace oneself. This could be a company involved in manufacturing, but could also be a shop, a restaurant, a hairdresser's or a massage clinic.

48 Højrup 1983.

3 Labour Market Strategies

Unemployment

According to Saskia Sassen, the preconditions for the development of a "global city" in one of the former industrial centres are the existence of a highly-developed infrastructure and public service system, a well-educated labour force which has lost its political power because manufacturing companies have closed and many people are unemployed, and a local government eager to attract investment. A decisive factor for development to take place is a change in the fixing of the level of wage costs. Sassen mentions that weakening of the trade unions is a condition for revaluation of the labour force purely on the basis of supply and demand. In the USA this has led to an extreme reduction in levels of pay for the lowest paid groups in the service sector. The reduction has gone so far that in some cases wage-earners are forced to work for wages that do not allow them to reproduce themselves. Young people at McDonalds, for instance, receive so little that they cannot afford a fair standard of living unless (for instance) they live more or less free with their parents or relatives. This has given us the concept of "the working poor", meaning people who, despite being employed, cannot rise out of poverty.

In the Danish Ministry for Industry's Trade Report 1994 it is recognised that there are significant employment opportunities in consumer services, but American conditions are undesirable:

"The USA has managed to create millions of jobs in consumer services, but the price is very low incomes. Denmark will not pursue that road. The choice must not be between being working poor and unemployment. The challenge in industrial policy is therefore to create scope for growth

41

and employment in the consumer services while ensuring fair pay for wage-earners."[1]

Precise instructions as to how to *create the possibility for growth and employment in consumer services while ensuring fair pay to wage-earners* are not given. The question, which need not only to be limited to consumer services but which can be formulated more generally, is: how can scope for growth and employment be created while ensuring fair pay to wage-earners? This is a big question, which has occupied researchers and politicians for years.

Irrespective of basic ideological views, the consensus is that the relatively high level of unemployment that has existed since the 1970s is a problem. However as soon as the problem must be defined, opinions polarise. In the following I will try to clarify this polarisation against the background of the Danish discussion.

At the neo-liberal pole, unemployment is seen as a problem because it puts a strain on society. Unemployment means increased taxes; it limits the individual tax-payer's private economic means; it increases moonlighting, etc. At the opposite, socialist pole, unemployment is considered a problem for society just as much as for the people forced into the stigmatising role of being unemployed. The increased pressure from taxes provokes negative attitudes in many taxpayers towards the State and those individuals who enjoy the benefits of social welfare payments.[2] The unwillingness of many tax-payers to contribute through taxation to collective welfare arrangements leads to the acceptance, and possibly even the desire, to reject the needy and thus, as the final consequence, to terminate the welfare model.[3]

The former group of researchers and liberal politicians in Denmark have managed to create a discourse,[4] which has dominated the public debate. It asserts that *there should be no disincentive to work*. Unemployment benefit and other social payments are too high, and many unemployed people are so because they cannot be bothered to find work when they will not get much more out of working than they do from social benefits. Unemployment is therefore voluntary.

In the following I will try to show that this notion is built on phrases and dogmata, which do not correspond to reality but which still have a powerful effect because the people who maintain this is reality believe in them and act in accordance with them.

Researchers who pay homage to *there should be no disincentive to work* perceive the unemployment problem from a narrow viewpoint, seen from a social scientific angle, since they primarily focus on the supply side. They only see half the picture of reality since unemployment is not just a question of a glut of labour on the market but also a question of lack of demand. The unemployment problem has two sides: a supply side and a demand side, and seen scientifically it is unsatisfactory to focus on one side only because this blocks wider understanding.

The inequality strategy

The Head of Research at the Rockwool Foundation's Research Unit, Gunnar Viby Mogensen, asserts that the Danish welfare state model is in crisis.[5] He justifies this by the fact that in 1990 Denmark spent 60% of the GNP on public expenditure and social payments, compared for instance with 45% in Germany and 36% in the USA.[6] At the same time he points out that the burden of providing for the non-working section of the Danish population is unchanged. In 1970 and in 1992, 70-72% of the population in the active age group were in employment. In 1970, provision for the non-working section of the Danish population occurred within the family, while in 1992 a significant proportion of the redistribution took place outside the framework of the family through the public purse.[7] In 1970, approximately 7% of the total population depended on social income support. This figure had risen to 24% in 1992 and forecasts of population development show that, if welfare arrangements are not altered, the burden of support will rise even further.[8]

Viby Mogensen and a number of his colleagues with a dominant influence on the discourse in Denmark regard unemployment as a serious economic burden for society, and they have expended a lot of energy and thinking to develop ideas to bring down taxes and duties in order to avoid the unfortunate side-effects they believe are linked with the present system. They consider the high tax burden to have a carry-over effect on the development of the informal economy and on do-it-yourself work. According to Professor Henrik Petersen another side-effect of high taxes is that individuals lose their freedom of choice and the opportunity to improve their own economic situation, and that the attempts of many people to escape from the trap through "black" activities etc., trigger reactions by the State. These take the form of new rules and sanctions, which in the end can develop into a control society.[9] The aim of society must therefore be to create employment and reduce the burden of taxation.

Since the middle 1980s, these researchers believed that unemployment is primarily caused by structural conditions.[10] They assert that there is no correlation between supply and demand as far as qualifications and/or their geographical distribution are concerned.[11] In this connection, they criticise the employment service and labour market training courses for being ineffective. They also say unemployment benefit is too high, making it difficult to find applicants for vacant positions. Many people lack any incitement to seek low-paid work because unemployment benefit amounts to 90% of their former income.

There should be no disincentive to work. Therefore there must be no barriers in the form of negotiated minimum levels of pay, and/or high private or public social welfare payments, which prevent free price-setting for labour. There must be an economic incitement to go to work. Therefore one must ask whether the private or public social insurance systems are not too high, so that they assure the unemployed a subsistence level above the market value of his labour.

Welfare policy provisions, i.e. provisions that ensure rights for employees in connection with, for instance, unemployment, illness, and pensions, or which affect groups of citizens who for one reason or another only have weak links to the labour market, can be organised in various ways. In many EU countries, the right to various welfare payments is achieved in relation to the individual's connection with the labour market. For example, German workers are ensured admission to the German hospital service through a medical insurance system paid for by the employer. In other countries, rights to social benefits are linked with citizenship. According to Due, Madsen and Jensen, one can differentiate between two types of welfare system: 1) those supported on the principles of insurance and 2) those where the right to welfare payments are linked to residence and citizenship.[12]

The latter model is typical of the Nordic countries, where social payments and rights in most areas are something citizens are entitled to automatically: everyone has the right to a pension, treatment under the health service, etc., irrespective of the links the individual has, or has had, to the labour market. In the other Continental countries the principle of insurance dominates. This means that the individual citizen must insure himself against illness, unemployment, old age, etc., and this insurance is normally linked to employment conditions. Social benefits are thus primarily attained by being insured, and the amount of the individual's social benefit is directly related to his links with the labour market so that a pension, for instance, will depend partly on how long the individual has worked during his lifetime and partly on how much the individual earned.[13]

Table 1:   **Direct taxes, indirect taxes (VAT, excise duty), other taxes and compulsory social contributions as a percentage of overall public taxation plus compulsory social contributions in the EU states, Norway and Sweden, in 1986**

	Indirect taxes	Direct taxes	Other taxes	Social contributions
Denmark	34.2	56.1	6.5	3.2
Belgium	22.2	40.3	3.7	33.7
France	28.3	18.1	10.9	42.8
Greece	41.4	17.4	8.4	32.7
Holland	23.7	27.6	6.1	42.3
Ireland	42.3	36.1	7.5	14.2
Italy	23.2	37.8	4.7	34.2
Luxembourg	24.0	43.2	7.1	25.7
Portugal	46.6	21.3	4.0	28.1
Spain	31.6	25.0	4.3	39.1
Germany	23.7	34.7	4.3	37.3
UK	29.0	38.2	14.9	17.9
Sweden	23.6	42.8	8.6	25.0
Norway	37.6	36.1	4.0	22.3
EU	30.5	34.0	6.8	28.8

Source: Due, Madsen and Jensen 1992: 31.

These two systems manifest themselves in differing pay structures. As shown in Table 1, employers' social contributions constituted only 3.2% of combined taxes plus mandatory social contributions in Denmark in 1986. In France this figure was 42.8%, in Holland 42.3% and in Germany 37.3%.

In countries where the social contributions are only a limited amount, it can hardly pay employers to devise methods of evading payment, while the motivation to undertake such actions is greater in countries where mandatory social contributions are significantly higher. At the same time "tax considerations" can appear, i.e. attempts to evade taxation.

An example appears, therefore, in Portugal, where in recent years green cards have been issued liberally to employees whereby they are considered as self-employed and are thus personally responsible for payment of taxes and social insurance. If they fail to insure themselves, they can afford to work for wages below the norm. The same applies to English labourers who register as self-employed and work in Germany.

The basic idea of the State-financed social welfare society is that the State will care for individuals who are in need. The help is financed through taxation.

Viby-Mogensen and many other economists in Denmark and the other EU countries do not consider that the reasons for the persistent unemployment in the majority of EU countries are primarily based on a decline in demand, since if this were so it would be expected that an automatic adjustment would bring back a lower level of unemployment over the course of time. To explain why this has not occurred, the hysteresis theory was devised at the end of the 1980s. This postulates that a rise in unemployment, e.g. as a result of a fall in demand, will tend to become permanent because it is only the employed (insiders) that take part in pay negotiations. They exert pressure to improve their pay and conditions without considering the needs of the unemployed (outsiders). It is thought they are often successful in taking advantage of this situation because they know it costs an employer a great deal to recruit and train new hands. This forces the employees' pay up to levels far above their true market value, and this automatically contributes to keeping the unemployed from getting work, resulting in higher, persistent unemployment.[14]

One possible effect of the hysteresis theory is that the number of long-term unemployed will increase during a continuing recession, and the qualifications of the unemployed will fall, just as the long-term unemployed may, in time, become demoralised and give up seeking employment. When the upswing comes, the effective labour supply will have been permanently reduced, and the economy will not automatically return to its original situation. The negative pressure of unemployment on the tempo of pay rises is reduced, since the long-term unemployed have no real influence on wage agreements.[15]

The barrier to development, according to these researchers, is the way in which the system of daily unemployment allowances in Denmark has been organised.[16] The effect on a member of an unemployment fund is no different, whether there are 10,000 unemployed or 300,000. Each member of the fund pays the same contribution irrespective of the number of unemployed, since the State covers the remaining amount. State expenditure in connection with the daily unemployment allowance is financed through taxation, the burden thus being spread between everyone, becoming nearly invisible. Were it only those in employment who had to bear the whole burden, they would immediately be able to see and feel a relief in their contributions to the unemployment funds if more people came into employment. This could create an incitement among the employed to get the unemployed back to work.

This might even motivate the trade unions to get more unemployed back to work.[17] Jensen, Schmidt-Sørensen and Smith believe that the proportion of unemployed could be brought down to around 5% through a direct attack on the marginalisation processes and the mechanisms of hysteresis. This would require a clearer division of efforts between the labour market's parties on the one side and the State on the other, with the labour market parties primarily ensuring a fixed allocation of wages in relation to the labour force's true market value, the political objectives for distribution being undertaken through fiscal and social policies.

The neo-liberal economists also propose the introduction of productivity-linked pay for young people without training or work experience, the abolition of collectively agreed minimum pay levels, and the reduction of the daily allowance period. In order to compensate for the greater inequality in distribution, the authorities must step in with measures "which should, however, be formulated so that they do not damage incitements to seek employment".[18] Long-term unemployed over the age of 50, with few prospects for lengthy employment before retirement, should be offered an early retirement scheme, and the remaining poorly placed groups must receive a minimum income guaranteed by the public authorities. This means that by abolishing the minimum level of pay and forcing numbers of people to work for extremely low wages, the authorities must supplement up to a fixed minimum income.

Clearly the goal is to give employers on the private labour market the opportunity to engage people for what is called "their actual market value" and let the public authorities act as backstop and ensure everyone a minimum income from the public purse.[19]

Other neo-liberal researchers have proposed the development of a low-pay area by giving tax relief to people in employment on part of their income. An allowance of 10% of earned income up to DKK 130,000 has been suggested. This would mean a loss in income for the state, but would, it is said, give, "the weakest in the labour market the ability to sell themselves at their actual market value without going down in total income".[20] Lars Haagen Petersen, senior lecturer at Copenhagen University, sees several advantages in "employment tax relief". 1) It will keep pay down, especially for the low-paid; 2) "employment tax relief" should not be given to the unemployed. Therefore the advantage of exchanging benefits for fixed employment would be greater; 3) numbers of new jobs would arise. These are service jobs that employers no longer advertise because they know that nobody will be interested. So "employment tax relief" would in many ways have a reasonable effect on the employment of the lowest-paid.[21]

The idea that *there should be no disincentive to work* has also led the neo-liberal researchers to focus on the question of whether a new daily unemployment allowance culture has arisen? Do the unemployed misuse the daily unemployment allowance system by accepting daily allowances without really being interested in working? On the basis of a major questionnaire, Peder Pedersen and Nina Smith have tried to clarify the unemployed's own attitude to unemployment in relation to the demands contained in the various availability requirements. They asked about frequency in applying for jobs, willingness to commute, pay requirements, etc., and found that many did indeed want to work. At the same time they refer to other studies, which have shown that 43% of those who have been unemployed for more than three months do not object to being, unemployed for a longer period, provided they receive benefits. They conclude, "Even though it is hard to put precise figures on the discussion of a daily unemployment allowance culture or real unemployment, it can be concluded that it is a problem there is an incitement structure which means that some people must take money to work with them. It is similarly problematic for long-term respect for daily unemployment allowances if it largely becomes to a question of 'help yourself' system".[22]

The perspective of the investigation is very narrow, as the two researchers neglected to study a number of important factors. For instance they asked a lot about the interviewee's age, sex, family circumstances, etc., but did not ask how many times he or she had run into a brick wall when seeking work. Thus they failed to try to gain a picture of the unemployed person's personal experience. At the end of the 1980s, I interviewed a number of people between 18 and 30 about their view of the unemployed and, if they were unemployed, how they experienced their own and other unemployed people's situation.[23] The results of my study can be interpreted to show that people are affected by their experience and need a positive view of themselves, and that the interview in which they are taking part plays a decisive roll to the answers they give. Pedersen and Smith did not try to ascertain whether many possibly regard having work as a privilege even though, measured purely in cash, it does not give them much more than the daily unemployment allowance. There are many social benefits connected with having a job compared with being "unemployed", which is socially stigmatising. One could wish that Pedersen and Smith had gone a little further in their questioning and opened the way to a wider understanding. As the former Danish Minister of Social Affairs so rightly asked: "Are we counting what counts?".[24]

Belief in the dogma that *there should be no disincentive to work* also leads neo-liberal researchers to look more closely at whether the level of the daily unemployment allowance is too high, removing the economic incitement which in their opinion is necessary for going to work. Compared with most other EU States, Denmark has developed quite a generous system of welfare arrangements, especially unemployment benefit, social payments and social pensions. At best, the unemployed can achieve support corresponding to 90% of their former wages, though not more than 90% of the average wage on the private labour market covered by collective bargaining. This caused economists Pedersen and Smith to think that workers at the lower end of the pay scale have rightly been able to ask themselves whether there is an economic incentive to work.[25]

The question of whether there is an economic incentive to work if one, as unemployed, can receive passive public support only 10% under what one receives when working resulted in an extensive questionnaire investigation performed by the Rockwool Foundation in 1993-1994. The study shows that, among those at work, 3% of men and 8% of women "lost" disposable income by going to work, while about 17% earned less than DKK 500 a month extra by working instead of being fully unemployed on daily unemployment allowance.[26] According to the study some 28% of the working Danish population had no great economic benefit from going to work. Instead of asking this 28% why they go to work, Pedersen and Smith ask themselves this question, and give the following answer:

"This can be due to the fact that many have difficulty in finding out about the many different regulations in the tax, daily unemployment allowance and benefit systems, so that they have not found whether it can actually pay to work. It may also be that many people do not want to 'exploit' the system, either because of their opinions, or moral arguments, or because receiving public support is still as shameful. It might also be due there being many non-economic incitements to work, such as social contacts, a structured daily life, fringe benefits, etc."[27]

Pedersen and Smith did not take the trouble to investigate the validity of their conclusions. How many Danes are so stupid that they do not know whether it cannot pay to work or not? How many Danes do not want to exploit the system on the basis of their opinions or moral arguments? And why do they hold these opinions and moral arguments?

The only thing Pedersen and Smith can conclude definitely is that there are, in fact, many Danes who work, even though they do not get much money out of it. What it is that keeps them going, Pedersen and Smith did not take the trouble to ask. It would have been quite simple to follow these questions up, but they chose to base their conclusions on their own definition of reality.

It is not only in Denmark that neo-liberal researchers have tried to influence the discourse. The same applies to other EU States.[28] According to Lind, it is a widely held belief that lack of flexibility in the labour market is the cause of most of the structural unemployment in Europe, and that labour market reforms should be implemented in the form of increased flexibility, decentralisation, education, training and an active employment policy. To reduce unemployment and strengthen economic growth, greater flexibility in pay and conditions must be created. This should be brought about through a reduction in unemployment benefit and social support, removal of trade union barriers, and an active labour market policy to include training and work instead of unemployment benefit, and a strengthening of State placement services.[29]

According to the neo-liberal researchers this can, among other things, be brought about by decentralising collective bargaining so that the market determines pay levels to a greater extent, while benefits are reduced and/or the financing of unemployment insurance is re-organised so that groups with a high risk of unemployment pay the marginal costs themselves. In this way the unemployed could choose between a combination of lower pay, lower risk of unemployment and lower contributions to unemployment insurance, and a combination of higher pay, high risk of unemployment and, in consequence, higher contributions to unemployment insurance.

Seen theoretically, the proposers perform theoretical circularism by asserting that unemployment among "outsiders" is due to their low productivity compared with the payment they could receive if they were employed. The "proof" should be that everyone in employment who receives wages has a productivity, which at least corresponds to their pay, otherwise they would not be employed. This is the same as saying that all unemployed do not have productivity high enough to pay for what they demand. The "proof" that this is correct is that they are unemployed.[30]

Despite thorough research over the last 40 years, it has not been possible for the neo-liberal researchers to obtain positive empirical proof of any connection between the financing of unemployment benefits, the level of support, pay, and employment. Despite assertions that assumptions on structural unemployment are based on objective economic analyses, it has not been possible to document the necessary connection. Nevertheless, it is asserted that increased flexibility in relation to pay will create more jobs. This is possible, but in order to create increased economic growth by attracting certain types of industry, pay must be reduced to a level where it can compete with countries where wages are extremely low. In the textile industry, Denmark has lost many jobs to countries where seamstresses earn a day's pay frequently 5 to 10 times under the collective agreed minimum pay in Denmark. In order to attract these jobs back to Denmark, Danish seamstresses will be forced to take employment at even lower wages than the seamstresses abroad, and this will not ensure them a reasonable standard of living seen with Danish eyes.[31] The result will probably be that Denmark, like the USA, will develop a phenomenon like "the working poor" with its social consequences of increased violence, crime and drug abuse, and increased demands for law and order, which contain a threat to democracy.

Full employment

The fact that it has not been possible to obtain positive empirical proof of a connection between the financing of unemployment benefit, the level of support, pay and employment ought to worry the neo-liberal researchers and cause them to consider critically whether the dogma that *there should be no disincentive to work* is valid at a time of high unemployment, where work itself has become a privilege. Where Viby Mogensen sees it as a crisis that the burden of support has not changed for several decades, where 70-75% of the active age group have supported the rest of the population at the same time as the State has increasingly taken over support of the remainder, this is not necessarily a direct indication of crisis. The fact that the State increasingly ensures unemployed people and pensioners a fair economic basis for their existence has resulted in these people no longer being totally dependent on their relatives' charity and ability to support them. Danish society has moved towards an increasing share of tasks formerly performed in individual households now being undertaken by public or private institutions, where they are performed professionally. This has created increased social security and confidence for those in need. For children and young people today who come into day-care institutions there is a greater opportunity for social contact with other children and young people under professional supervision and for a greater number of activities than if they stayed at home being looked after by an au pair girl or their mother. This means that the tax burden increases, but to see it as a crisis can only imply the wish to return to "the good old days". The fact that Denmark has been able to manage quite well economically in relation to the countries with which we normally compare ourselves should be taken as a positive sign, especially since there has been significant unemployment, that 28% of people go to work without it paying them economically, and that the tax burden is heavy.

The claim that wage increases are caused by a shortage of labour, which is a mainstay in the assertion that the labour market has structural problems, is not necessarily correct. As Lind has correctly pointed out, there can be many reasons for wage increases, for instance companies earning large profits, trade unions managing to push wage demands through, etc. Before these reasons are explained, it is impossible to say anything definite about structural unemployment.[32]

As far as the insider-outsider theory is concerned, this is not valid. Wage-setting in the 1980s, according to Lind, was also extremely flexible, with wide scope for the individual employer to differentiate between core and peripheral labour. Moreover, as stated, the hysteresis theory suffers from tautology and circularism.[33] In countries where so-called structural problems are fewer than in Denmark, experience has not been convincing towards a reduction in unemployment. This is true, for instance, in England, where the weekly unemployment benefit is approximately equal to the amount received per day in Denmark, and where no significant fall in unemployment has taken place despite massive privatisation and laws to restrict the powers of the trade unions.[34]

The argument of the neo-liberals that most unemployment is due to structural problems caused by too high wages and daily unemployment allowances etc., is a consequence of their focusing exclusively on the supply side of the labour market: unemployment is the unemployed person's own fault because he asked for too much in wages, had the wrong qualifications and, did not want to work because unemployment benefits was too high.

It is also necessary to look at the demand side. Companies play a part in developments in the labour market, and therefore also contribute to the appearance of bottlenecks and structural problems. It is management in companies who decide on segmentation, flexibility, allocation and qualification. Structural problems often arise because companies do not consciously and responsibly look after and cater for the labour market. Through their organisations, companies can influence the committees and tribunals who arrange and control occupational training and can thus prevent bottlenecks.

At certain times and in certain areas, demand can naturally arise for particular qualifications that cannot immediately be covered, even though unemployment is generally high, but this is hardly the most serious problem in a labour market with more than 10-12% unemployed. The problem is not primarily lack of qualifications but the presence of surplus and unused qualifications. By focusing mainly on the marginal over-demand for certain types of labour, the neo-liberal economists have coloured the discourse and contributed to a widespread belief that training can play a significant role in the solution of structural problems in the labour market.

Training the unemployed to perform jobs which may become vacant in companies and thus avoid possible bottlenecks is all very fine but, as Lind correctly points out, it has not been possible to document that this can have anything other than a marginal influence on unemployment. High unemployment is not caused by the majority of the unemployed lacking training or having received the wrong training. Unemployment is caused by there not being enough jobs in relation to supply. Despite the neo-liberal researcher's many contrived theories, there is no guarantee that a reduction in the level of pay and lower unemployment benefits will increase demand.

It is difficult to predict the effects of technological development, and a reduction of pay levels is not necessarily identical with companies needing labour with precisely those qualifications, which are available. Not all companies' cost and production structure depends purely on the cost of labour. There may be other factors, such as dividends, management, exchange rates, the cost of raw materials, prices of machinery, land and buildings, etc. Finally there is the disadvantage that companies may neglect to keep up with technological developments, with serious long-term consequences.

The neo-liberal researchers have launched a violent attack on the current structures and institutions on the Danish labour market. The assertion that many unemployed do not try to find work is just not true. Every time an ordinary job is advertised, companies receive hundreds of applications, which contradict the accusation that unemployment is voluntary. The allegation that comparatively favourable unemployment benefit only has negative consequences overlooks the fact that resistance to layoffs is more restricted with a good unemployment support system than under one that is less so. A socially acceptable standard of living thus not only has consequences for distribution but also great significance on economic growth.

According to Colin Crouch, countries with comparatively well-developed organisations and institutional relations between State, labour and employers managed relatively well during the crisis in the 1980s.[35] Market forces alone cannot abolish unemployment properly. It can only be reduced either by job-sharing, employing more people in the public sector or developing arrangements such as early retirement, educational leave, parental leave etc.

The dogma that *there should be no disincentive to work* is irreconcilable with market logic at a time of high unemployment, because it is work itself which has become a privilege. During periods of full employment, when it is easy to get work, it can be tempting to take a break, especially if unemployment benefit can provide nearly as much as one gets when working, but when work is in short supply it gets another status. Then the value of having a job rises. In neo-liberal-dominated thinking, one looks at the situation that labour is demanded. In periods of full employment this is true, and pay levels rise, but when the circumstances are reversed, pay levels fall or the existing level of pay is maintained. Some people are lucky to keep their jobs and their pay, but others are thrown into unemployment and get less. As an unemployed person, one has nothing to bargain over with an employer. The level of daily unemployment allowance is set politically and is not determined by the market.

In periods of high unemployment, employers are in a favourable situation. They can pick and choose for the same price, or even for less. Competition between workers and employers is temporarily set aside. It is now workers who compete among themselves for the same jobs. In terms of market logic, it can be expected that the costs of obtaining or keeping a job would rise. If unemployment benefit rose in this situation, the economic advantages of getting a coveted job would fall. In accordance with classical market logic it follows that the more a ware is in demand, the higher the price. According to the argument that *there should be no disincentive to work* therefore, unemployment benefit must be reduced. This is directly contradictory to classical market logic as it results in the demander being rewarded. When an employer demands labour and there is a shortage, it is not the demander who is rewarded but the worker, who gets higher wages. As Qvortrup says, the dogma that *there should be no disincentive to work* is irreconcilable with market logic at a time of high unemployment.[36]

The role of being unemployed has a high price even though, via comparatively high unemployment benefits, one may perhaps not suffer a noticeable financial loss. There are social costs connected with unemployment. Children are hard hit when parents are out of work for long periods. When the children grow up, 40% of them end up as unemployed, and they suffer from far more mental and physical complaints than children in working families. The risk of getting involved in crime is 20-30% greater for children of the long-term unemployed, while the risk of being removed from home is 90% greater than in other families. This is shown in an investigation performed by Mogens Christoffersen, who followed children born to long-term unemployed parents between 1966 and 1973.

The investigation also showed that even a single year's unemployment can lead to an increase in divorces, drug-related problems, suicide attempts and suicide among parents. In children it results in an increased likelihood of being admitted to hospital, attempted suicide and crime. The investigation shows that:

1) The longer unemployment continues, the more often social and health consequences for the children arise. Children inherit their parents' misery;
2) About 7% of children of long-term unemployed families have experienced one of their parents attempting or committing suicide. This is twice the national average;
3) About 12% of fathers are hospitalised for alcoholism. This is three times the average;
4) Around 3% of children have experienced one or both parents being exposed to violence and admitted to hospital. This is three times more often than their peers;
5) Every fifth father has been given an unconditional prison sentence. This is four times the average;
6) Psychiatric complaints arise twice as often; and
7) About a quarter of the children have experienced at least one of their parents being admitted to hospital for a mental condition or as a result of alcohol-related illness, attempted suicide or drug-addiction. This is twice as often as in other families.

All these factors give the children poorer living conditions, and the social inheritance is carried on when the children grow up. Long-term unemployment, therefore, has excessive human costs. In the investigation, the "long-term unemployed" were defined as people who had more than 25% unemployment at the time the children were teenagers. It followed 15,000 children of long-term unemployed parents.[37]

Notes

1 Trade Report 1994: 39.
2 It is precisely this which has contributed to a high degree to the development of the xenophobia which characterises many Danes (Hjarnø 1993, Schierup 1993).
3 Lind 1995: 183-185.
4 "Discourse has become a common term in the social sciences. Discourse means a collection of platitudes and concepts which together construe a subject in a certain way. The discourse supplies us with a particular language which contributes to the formation of our

knowledge, the moulding of our opinions and the strengthening of our actions" (Schierup 1993: 13-14).

5   Viby-Mogensen 1995: 20-21.

6   As far as Germany is concerned, he seems to ignore the fact that a realistic evaluation of pay levels ought also to include the mandatory employers' contributions to national insurance.

7   Viby-Mogensen could, for that matter, have gone right back to 1960 and shown that the employment rate for people between 15 and 64 years of age had been relatively stable at about 70-75%, and that employment had thus taken up the same percentage of the active age-group for 35 years. The actual labour force, however, has risen to 83% in 1994, and unemployment during the period 1960-1994 is mainly due to growth in participation, partly owing to more women becoming active and partly to a fall in activity among the younger and the elder. Much of the work formerly carried out by women in the home has been taken over by the public or private labour market (Ministry of Finance: Budget Report 95, Copenhagen 1995).

8   In 1994, nearly 25% of 15-64 year-olds received unemployment benefit or some other form of social payment in compensation for the lack of employment income. Less than half were registered as unemployed, so dependence on public support exceeds the registered level of unemployment. The group receiving public funds mainly because of unemployment includes, amongst others, the following groups in 1991: people on early retirement (257,000), voluntary early retirement arrangements (101,000), people receiving sickness benefit for more than 6 months of the year (120,000), people receiving social welfare payments for more than 6 months of the year (120,000) and people in job training arrangements (90,000) (Lind & Møller 1995: 9).

9   Petersen 1994: 2.

10 As well as the term structural unemployment, terms such as "recessional unemployment", "frictional unemployment" and "temporary layoffs" are also used. For a closer definition of these terms see Albæk, Madsen & Pedersen 1992: 24-29.

11 Structural unemployment is a phenomenon connected with the condition under which at a time with high unemployment there can be a lack of available labour within specialised trades or a particular geographical area. In the portion of the market where there is a lack of available labour, pay will rise if activities rise. "How far these shifts in demand on the labour market result in structural unemployment

depends on the professional and geographical mobility on the part of the supply. If this is poor, the structural problems can be serious. Here pay structure, amongst other things, plays a large role. If the pay structure is locked tight, the necessary incitements are not created for the employers and employees to solve these structural problems" (Albæk, Madsen & Pedersen 1992: 28-29).

12 Due, Madsen & Jensen 1992: 113-117.

13 Due, Madsen & Jensen 1992: 114. For a detailed description of the two models, see Andersen 1991.

14 Jensen, Schmidt-Sørensen & Smith 1992: 13-14.

15 Jensen, Schmidt-Sørensen & Smith 1992: 13.

16 The basic principles of the Danish insurance system for daily allowances has remained unaltered since it was established in 1907. Unemployment insurance is based on voluntary membership of an unemployment fund legally administered by an institution which nearly always has connections with a trade union. A major reform in the 1960s introduced the current principle of financing unemployment benefits through member's contributions and employers' contributions, the remainder comingng from the State. I.e. the State pays the fringe costs of growing unemployment. Another important reform was the increase in benefit to 90% of former pay with a general maximum of 90% of the average income. The third element was that the right to assign work was taken from the union unemployment organisations and given to the public labour exchanges.

17 Jensen, Schmidt-Sørensen & Smith 1992: 13-14.

18 Jensen, Schmidt-Sørensen & Smith 1992: 15.

19 The consequences of the proposal to let employees themselves bear the burden of unemployment benefit can lead to various reactions which have not been considered. It could, perhaps, lead to the trade union organisations becoming more motivated towards the establishment of new, extremely low-paid jobs in order to get the unemployed into employment, or possibly that more effort will be made to create a division of labour. This might lead to a general fall in pay for certain groups. The proposal can possibly also produce a radicalisation in the trade union movement to cause the Danish government to demand a

stop to both the legal and illegal labour currently found in EU states south of the Danish-German border. The effect of a redistribution in the financing of unemployment benefits could also have the effect that it weakened the trade union organisations because many people in secure employment would resign from the unemployment funds, unless membership was made mandatory and the unemployment funds amalgamated. The proposal contains, in any case, a challenge to the present system of collective bargaining.

20 Mimi Jakobsen, Minister of Trade, Politiken, Sunday 4th February 1996, Section 2, page 7.

21 Politiken, Sunday 4th February 1996, section 2, page 7.

22 Pedersen & Smith 1995: 61.

23 Hjarnø 1988.

24 Olesen 1995: 175.

25 Pedersen & Smith 1995: 31-44. See also: Plough 1994, Plovsing 1994, Petersen & Søndergaard 1994. It is funny that these researchers have not directly asked people why they work.

26 Among the unemployed, about 6% of men and 10% of women expect their total financial situation to deteriorate if they take a job, while 17% of men and 26% of women do not expect it to alter their economic situation (Pedersen & Smith 1995: 41-32).

27 Pedersen & Smith 1995: 42-43.

28 White paper (KOM (93) 700 Final edition).

29 Lind 1995: 186-188.

30 Lind.

31 Lind 1992.

32 Lind 1992.

33 Lind 1992: 126.

34 Lind 1992: 127; Jeppesen & Lind: 1991.

35 Crouch 1993: 278-283.

36 Information 17.9.1993.

37 Christoffersen 1996.

4 Comparison Between the USA and Denmark

The neo-liberal argument that greater pay differentials will increase employment is certainly correct, but if it is not possible at the same time to support high productivity and the ability to compete internationally, in itself employment is not a benefit. There is of course a high human price connected with long-term unemployment, but it is uncertain whether increased employment through the creation of inequality by reducing unemployment benefit is a sensible solution. There is an argument that greater inequality easily results in lower economic growth which, among other things, can be documented through a comparison of developments in Denmark and the USA.

In 1960, the USA had a per capita GNP of US$ 2,842, while the corresponding figure in Denmark was only US$ 1,275, i.e. under half that of the USA. By 1994 the figures were US$ 25,852 for the USA and US$ 28,222 for Denmark: i.e. Danes had overtaken citizens in the USA by more than US$ 2,000 per year. As far as working hours are concerned, it was with mixed emotions that Danes learned some time ago that a 40 hour working week had been introduced in the USA, while it was still 48 hours in Denmark. The situation has since been reversed: Danes have a shorter working day on average than Americans. Though there is some uncertainty in these calculations, Danes have a higher productivity than American citizens. During periods of unemployment, Danish workers can receive benefits corresponding to some 90% of a normal worker's pay for several years, and studies have shown that 28% of people working in Denmark have no great economic advantage in working compared with the amount they would receive from unemployment benefit and other social payments. Nevertheless, these people work hard and effectively, so that Denmark currently has the fourth highest per capita GNP only surpassed by Japan, Switzerland and Luxembourg.

Throughout the 1980s, the 10% poorest people in Denmark experienced a gain in real income, while the 10% poorest people in the USA suffered a considerable decline. Why are things going so much worse in the USA than in Denmark? Why has a marginalisation process not arisen, resulting in numbers of new, extremely low-paid jobs in the consumer service industry in Denmark? Why does the phenomenon of "the working poor" not appear in Denmark, despite Denmark having had considerable unemployment for many years?

Figure 2:   Trends in total employment 1960-1996, ratio 1960=100

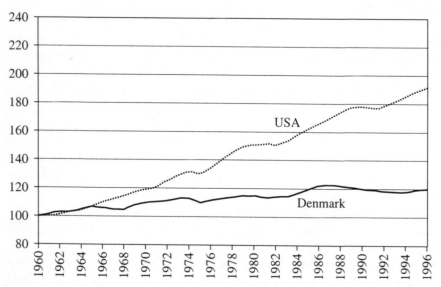

Source: Hjarnø, Jan 1996: 11.

As can be seen in Figure 2, comparison of expansion in employment and production per employee in the USA and Denmark from 1960 to 1996 shows that employment has risen much higher in the USA than in Denmark.[1] The weak increase in productivity in the USA suggests that much of the growth in employment has taken place in jobs with a low value increment, i.e. so-called "low quality" jobs.

The low growth in production per employee in the USA can be further illustrated by the fact that production per person of working age between 15 and 64 years rose slower in the USA than in Denmark, despite industrial and employment frequency rising significantly more in the USA than in Denmark during the period.

Figure 3: Trends in real GNP per employee, ratio in 1960=100

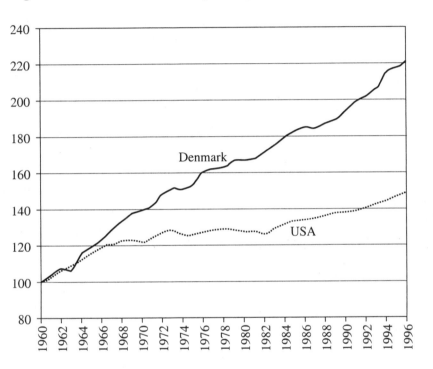

Source: Hjarnø, Jan 1996: 12.

As the Danish economist Bent Madsen pointed out, the US population is lagging further and further behind Denmark in terms of prosperity, even though the work force and employment have risen much more in the US than in Denmark.[2] Denmark has had a high, stable rate of employment of around 73% since 1960, while in the USA a strong rise in employment occurred, from about 60% in 1960 to the present level of around 73%.

Figure 4:   **Employment rate of total population between 15-64 years**

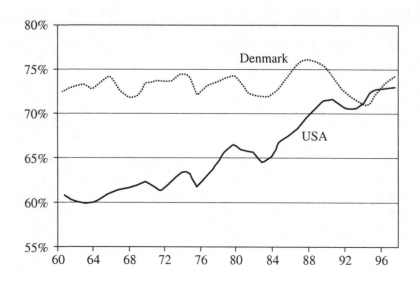

Source: Hjarnø, Jan 1996: 13.

There can be many reasons for the weak value increment in American jobs. Sassen points out amongst other things that it could be because the service sector has gained a dominant role in the USA, with many service jobs of low quality (low value increment), which are paid less than jobs in industry and agriculture. Compared with developments in Denmark, this theory cannot be confirmed.

Table 2 shows that the service sector share of employment is much higher in the USA than in Denmark, but the number of people employed in service industries actually rose slightly more in Denmark than in the USA between 1973 and 1993. These figures do not suggest that a rising number of employees in the service sector in the USA compared with Denmark can explain the relatively weaker growth in productivity in the USA. Categorised by sub-groups, there is also a high level of similarity between American and Danish developments in so far as the share of employment of the finance and welfare services rose greatly in both countries, while trade/catering and transport/communication rose the least.

Figure 5:   Real GNP per capita of total population between 15-64 years, ratio in 1960=100

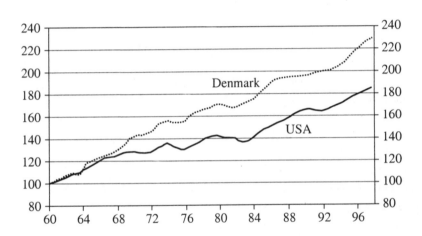

Source: Hjarnø, Jan 1996: 14.

There is, however, a clear difference between the USA and Denmark. Figure 6 shows that growth in the number of employees in the welfare services has largely occurred in the public sector in Denmark, while in the USA it has taken place in the private sector. In Denmark, high demands are made as to level of training and qualifications, which is not necessarily so to the same extent in the private sector in the USA. This may explain why there is a tendency towards low-quality jobs in the service sector in the USA.

The flourishing of so-called low-quality jobs in the USA is thus not, as Sassen has implied, exclusively due to a sector-shift in employment from manufacturing to the service sector.

Sassen has also pointed out that deregulation of the American employment market has led to many people not being able to find traditional full-time jobs. Table 3 shows that both the frequency of part-time work and the number of people in it against their will has been fairly constant in the USA and Denmark. Thus the weak growth in productivity in the USA cannot be directly explained by increased number of people in part-time employment.

Table 2:　Rate of employment distributed by sector

	USA			Denmark		
	Percentages of the total workforce					
	1973	**1993**	**Change**	**1973**	**1993**	**Change**
Agriculture, etc.	4.2	2.7	-1.5	9.5	5.2	-4.3
Industry	33.2	24.1	-9.1	33.8	26.3	-7.5
Service	62.6	73.2	10.6	56.7	68.4	11.7
of whom:						
- trade & catering	21.1	22.0	0.9	15.1	15.8	0.7
- transport & comm.	5.8	5.4	-0.4	7.0	7.2	0.2
- financial sector	7.3	10.9	3.6	5.9	10.1	4.2
- welfare services	28.5	34.9	6.4	28.2	34.6	6.4
- remainder				0.5	0.7	0.2

Source: OECD (1995) Labour Statistics, 1973-1993, from Bent Madsen, 1996.

Figure 6: **Proportion of public employees in relation to total number of employees[3]**

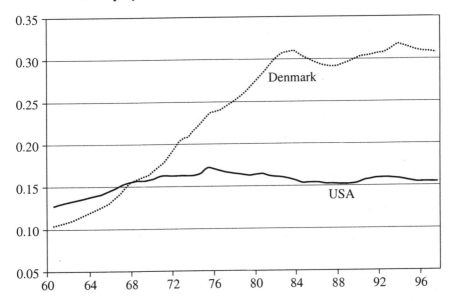

Source: Hjarnø, Jan 1996: 15.

Table 3:   Part-time frequency and involuntary part-time work

Part-time frequency	1973	1993
	Percentage of the workforce	
USA, both sexes	15.6	17.5
- Men	8.6	10.9
- Women	26.8	25.3
	1979	**1993**
Denmark, both sexes	22.7	23.3
- Men	5.2	11.0
- Women	46.3	37.3

Involuntary part-time	1983	1993
	Percentage of the workforce	
USA, both sexes	5.7	5.0
- Men	4.8	4.4
- Women	6.9	5.7
Denmark, both sexes	3.4	4.8
- Men	1.9	2.6
- Women	5.0	7.3

Source: OECD (1995), Employment Outlook, July 1995, from Bent Madsen 1996.

As a reason for the low wages in the service sector, Sassen points out that the growing participation rate of women lowers productivity, because women are employed in low productivity jobs, and they have a high part-time frequency and lower standard of education than men. As shown above, the first two arguments are irrelevant in relation to the weaker growth in affluence in the USA compared with Denmark.

From 1973 to 1993, a major increase took place in the rate of women's participation in the USA, from nearly 50% to around 65%. The increasing occupational participation of women might have put a downward pressure on male productivity, but it must have increased production per person in the population between 15 and 64 years of age, because women who come onto the labour market presumably contribute positively to production. Women's major increasing participation rate in the USA cannot therefore explain the generally weaker growth in affluence - *au contraire*.

Table 4:   Employment in relation to the potential workforce

	1973	1983	1993
USA			
- Men	82.8	76.5	79.0
- Women	48.0	56.1	64.4
Denmark			
- Men	89.0	78.3	77.9
- Women	61.2	65.0	69.6

The potential work force is defined as the number of people between 15 and 64 years of age.
Source: OECD (1995), Employment Outlook, July 1995, from Bent Madsen 1996.

Table 5:   Self-employed and assisting spouse, excluding agriculture

	1973	1993
	Percentage of the workforce	
USA	7.0	7.7
Denmark	10.9	7.7

Source: OECD (1995), Labour Force Statistics, 1995, from Bent Madsen 1996.

Sassen has also pointed out that the low-pay sector may be associated with the fact that numbers of self-employed in the USA have increased greatly. The hypothesis is that a large part of the increase in employment in the USA has occurred in the form of an increase in the number of self-employed, who support themselves by various kinds of low-productivity jobs. Statistics disprove this hypothesis (Table 5). The number of self-employed outside agriculture lay at the same low level in Denmark and the USA in 1993, but developments have been significantly different. The number of self-employed in the USA increased by nearly 0.7% of the work force from 1973 to 1993, while in Denmark fell by more than 3%. This development could have contributed to higher growth in productivity in Denmark compared with the USA, because enterprises with low productivity normally disappear due to competition.

Developments in income distribution

As Sassen has correctly pointed out, it is difficult to measure income distribution in one country, and even harder to make dependable comparisons of these figures between two countries as differently organised as the USA and Denmark. Despite this, it is possible to show that income distribution in the USA is far more unequal than in Denmark. By looking at the so-called Gini coefficient, which indicates the share of total income that must be redistributed for income distribution to be totally equal, it is possible to gain an impression of income distribution. Table 6 shows the Gini coefficient for gross income for men working full time all year. In 1986, 29.8% of the total income in the USA would need to be redistributed in order to achieve an even distribution, and this is 4% higher than in 1979 when the coefficient was 25.8%. The corresponding figures for Denmark were 18.2% in 1987 and 16.2% in 1981.

Table 6:   **Gini coefficients for gross payment for men, working full time all year**

	USA		Denmark	
	1986	29.8	1987	18.2
	1979	25.8	1981	16.2
Difference		4.0		2.0

Gini coefficients indicate the share of total income which must be redistributed for incomes to be equal.
Source: Petersen (1994), op. cit., p. 9, from Bent Madsen 1996.

These figures show that income distribution was much more unequal in the USA than in Denmark in the 1980s. In both countries there was a tendency for income distribution to become even more unequal in the course of the 1980s, the trend being stronger in the USA.

Table 7 shows an OECD calculation of relative poverty before and after tax and benefit. The figures show that there is a significant levelling of income distribution through taxes and social payments in Denmark, while the levelling in the USA is highly limited. The high degree of income levelling in Denmark is especially due to social payments. Income tax has only a modest effect, while indirect taxes pull in the direction of greater inequality.

Table 7:   Relative poverty before and after taxes and benefits

	Before tax and social benefits	After tax and social benefits	Relative degree of compensation
	(Percentage of population in poor families)		
Denmark	20.2	5.7	-71.8
USA	19.4	18.7	-3.6

The income expression used is the annual household income divided by the members of the household. The level of unemployment, social development, amount of part-time work, number of family members under 18, etc., is thus significant for this expression.
The relative poverty level is defined as 50% of median income.
The relative degree of compensation is calculated as the relative change in the numbers of the population in poor families.
Source: OECD, Economic Surveys, Denmark 1996, p. 60, from Bent Madsen 1996.

Before tax and social payments, the proportion of poor people is of roughly the same order in the USA and Denmark.[4]

Figure 7:   Trends in income dispersal 1973-1991 in the USA and Denmark[5]

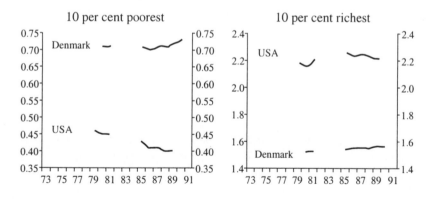

Source: Hjarnø, Jan 1996: 20.

Figure 7 shows the development in income spread during the period 1973 to 1991 for gross earnings of both sexes for incomes of the 10% poorest and the 10% richest measured in relation to the middle income. There is a marked difference between the USA and Denmark: the spread in incomes is much less in Denmark than in the USA. The lowest 10% earn a lot less than the middle income groups in the USA than in Denmark, and the rich in Denmark earn less, compared with the middle income group, than the rich in the USA.

The poorest 10% have become even poorer in the USA, while developments in Denmark have been in the direction of a narrowing of income differences. For the 10% richest, the development was less marked in both countries.

Figure 8:   Trends in real income distributed by deciles, ratio in 1980=100[6]

10 per cent poorest   Middle income   10 per cent richest

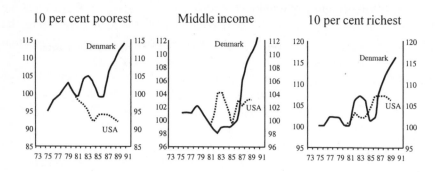

Source: Hjarnø, Jan 1996: 21.

The loss of terrain by the poor in the income race in the USA has had serious consequences, because the growth in prosperity in the USA has generally moved very slowly. The poorest 10% thus experienced a reduction in real income of nearly 10% from 1980 to 1989 in the USA, while the same group in Denmark experienced a rise in real income of 14% (Figure 8). Both middle and high income groups in the USA experienced a rise in real income throughout the 1980s, but this was been modest compared with real income development in Denmark for the corresponding income groups.

The consequence of the growing inequality in the USA has among other things been the appearance of the phenomenon of "the working poor" and a low economic growth rate.

Inequality gives lower growth

Henrik Hoffman has recently drawn attention to a number of interesting international articles in which, by analysing the relationships between economic growth and developments in income distribution, the main conclusion reached is that *greater inequality results in lower economic growth.*[7]

In 1994, Torsten Persson and Guido Tabellini published two different empirical analyses in which they tried to explain the development in economic growth per inhabitant with the aid of the level of GNP at the starting point, an expression for education, and a variable showing income distribution.[8]

In their first analysis, nine countries were included: Austria, the United Kingdom, Denmark, Finland, Germany, Holland, Norway, Sweden and the USA, in which they looked at the period from the mid-1800s to 1985. As an expression of inequality of income, they calculated how large a share of income before tax the 20% best placed in the population had. The higher this figure, the greater the inequality in incomes is considered to be. The analysis shows that the variable for income distribution is statistically significant for the level of economic growth rates over a very long period. The result is that the more unequal income distribution is, the less the economic growth per inhabitant.

The difference in income distribution alone explains a fifth of the changes in economic growth rates between countries and over time. Moreover the result can be interpreted such that if the richest fifth of the population had their total income increased by 10-15 per cent points, the total economic growth would be reduced by about 0.5 per cent points a year.

In the other analysis, Persson and Tabellini look at the period 1960-1985 and include 56 countries, both developed and less developed ones. They again try to explain the development of economic growth per inhabitant by, among other things, income distribution. The variable for income distribution here is how large a share the middle five per cent of all households have of the total income. The average share is 13.3%. Denmark is definitely above this, while e.g. African lands are generally a long way under. Inequality is considered to be able discernible through the small share of income in the middle 5% of the population.

The results of the analysis are clear. The more unequal income distribution is before tax, the lower the economic growth. The analysis can be interpreted so that if income distribution before tax is changed to increase the middle 5% of households' income share by 25-30% at the cost of the richest part of the population, the result would be an increase in GNP growth per inhabitant of 0.5% per year.

Alberto Alesina and Dani Rodrik have similarly tried to explain the level of growth per inhabitant from various measurements of inequality, the initial starting point for prosperity level and an education variable.[9] They investigate two periods, 1960-1985 and 1970-1985, by looking at two variables in income distribution, the Gini coefficients for income distribution and property distribution respectively. The Gini coefficient indicates the share of total income to be reallocated for income distribution to be totally equal, and is thus a combined measurement for the degree of inequality. The more unequal the distribution is, the greater the Gini coefficient, i.e. the more must be reallocated to give all an equal amount.

For both periods of analysis, the conclusion is that both property distribution and income distribution have a statistically significant effect in relation to explaining the level of economic growth. The greater the Gini coefficient, i.e. the more unequally incomes and fortunes are divided, the lower the economic growth per inhabitant.

Birdsall, Ross and Sabot, too, looked at the connection between inequality and growth.[10] Their target is to explain why during the last three decades a number of Southeast Asian countries had an economic growth above far that of the majority of countries in South America, despite the fact that the starting point for the two regions was not widely different at the beginning of the 1960s.

The three researchers argue that a significant difference in the growth performance of the two regions has been that in Southeast Asia there was a comparatively low level of inequality in the previous period. An important way of achieving this at the same time as having high economic growth was that among other things they focused more on the political area, which "spread" the growth and thereby reduced poverty and income opportunities. There were land reforms, investment in improvement of the infrastructure in country areas and, not least, a broad educational programme. South Korea and Venezuela were compared, inter alia. In the mid 1980s there was no great difference between the two countries in public contributions to education. However in Venezuela nearly 45% was spent on the higher education sector, against only 10% in South Korea. In societies with very unequal incomes, the possibilities for education are also unevenly divided. The richest get most here, too, which is not beneficial to combined growth potential. The conclusion is that inequality contributes negatively to economic growth. Correspondingly, it is confirmed that a broad educational effort is an important means of reducing inequality.

The authors illustrate the meaning of inequality and education with a number of calculations. They arrive at the conclusion that if in 1960 South Korea had had an equally low educational level as Pakistan, for instance, that alone would have meant that the gross national product per inhabitant in the middle 1980s would have been 40.5% lower in South Korea. Similarly, growth in South Korea would have 0.7% points lower each year from 1960 to 1985, if South Korea had had Brazil's level of inequality in incomes in 1960.

These new empirical analyses of the connection between growth, education and inequality over a number of long time-horizons demonstrate that there can be economic disadvantages in an inequality strategy. This also appeared in my comparison between development in the USA and Denmark. The neo-liberal Danish economist's arguments for increasing pay differentials and reducing unemployment benefit and social payments contain a threat that could lead Denmark along a path leading to American conditions.[11]

Notes

1   Madsen 1996.
2   Madsen 1996.
3   Source: Economic Outlook Bank, no. 58. from Bent Madsen 1996.
4   This seems to be in conflict with the conclusion in Table 6, where the Gini coefficient for gross income for men is around 10% points greater in the USA than in Denmark. An explanation for this discrepancy may be that low-income groups in Denmark comprise a comparatively large number of pensioners, people receiving early retirement allowance, and unemployed with no occupational income, but the corresponding groups in the USA are apparently still in the employment market and receive occupational income.
5   Comment: The figures for both countries is gross earnings per hour for both sexes. Systems with an annual bonus, such as the 13. monthly

salary in the USA, is included. Source: OECD (1993), Trends in earnings dispersion, 1973-91: 159-61, Economic Outlook, July 1993.

6   Comment: The figures for Denmark do not start before 1980. OECD (1993), Trends in earnings dispersion, 1973-91: 159-61, Economic Outlook, July 1993. From Bent Madsen 1996.

7   Hoffman 1996.

8   Persson & Tabellini 1994: 600-621.

9   Alesina & Rodrik 1994: 465-485.

10   Birdsall, Ross & Sabot 1995: 477-508.

11   See also OECD 1997.

5   Effects of Economy

The effects of long-term unemployment

A matter that has not been considered in the unemployment debate is social actors' response to unemployment seen in relation to their lifestyle. As long as a State maintains a high level of social welfare in a situation where the supply of labour exceeds demand, it can be considered as long-term public support. It is my hypothesis that such support will have different effects on the unemployed, depending on the lifestyle, which characterises them. Instead of just counting heads, as is normally done when calculating unemployment, perhaps the social actor's various social identities in relation to lifestyle should be taken into consideration.

People characterised by the wage-earner's lifestyle regard work as a necessity to obtain the money they need to live life in their leisure time. If they have developed a set of leisure activities, individuals like these will be able to manage a life of unemployment as long as public support in the form of unemployment benefit or early retirement arrangements is not much lower than the income they would have received if in a job. However, they would suffer the social stigma of being long-term unemployed.

In a period of high unemployment, work is not just a privilege in economic terms but also socially, which is why there is an absolute incitement to take employment. Unemployment contains a threat of impossibility of regaining a foothold in the labour market. The longer one is unemployed, the harder it is to get a job; amongst other things, one's qualifications suffer from lack of use. Numerous studies have shown that having work is considered positive, whilst it is considered extremely taxing to be excluded. Having a job confers prestige. There is a loss of prestige in relation to colleagues, family, friends and neighbours in being unemployed. For many people, it is humiliating to be dependent on public funds. Unemployment is a strain on one's health; it affects many people both mentally and physically. Unemployment damages the quality of life. Children suffer from their parents being unemployed; it is demeaning in relation to their friends. It also lessens the opportunities for saving up for a pension to ensure security in old age.[1] For an individual with a wage-earner lifestyle, there are many non-economic incitements to have and keep a job.

For people with a careerist lifestyle, where the goal in life is to make a career, unemployment can be extremely onerous, not just economically but especially because unemployment can block their career.[2] In one way unemployment takes away the whole meaning of life for these social actors, and they are hit by exactly the same socially stigmatising factors as people with a wage-earner lifestyle.

For people with a self-employed lifestyle, their goal in life is existence as independently self-employed. For individuals with this social identity, it can be hard to come to terms with a passive existence as unemployed. Individuals with a self-employed lifestyle very often have few special leisure interests. For many independent self-employed people, their firm is their only interest and it can be very difficult for them to pass the time and come to terms with a passive existence as unemployed, because life unemployed has no meaning. These are often people for whom the hourly rate of pay does not play a large role as long as by putting in a day (often a long one) in their own firm they can ensure an income on which they can live, and who expect their economic situation to improve. It can therefore be expected that unemployed people with a self-employed lifestyle will try to break out of idleness by establishing themselves as self-employed if possible.

People with a self-employed lifestyle have been fed with get-up-and-go and vitality with their mother's milk. It is not known how many people in Denmark have a self-employed lifestyle, but the number has been declining for many years, leading to fewer children and young people than formerly being influenced in childhood by their parents being self-employed. It will probably also result in fewer young people themselves having a self-employed lifestyle.

In a post-industrial society, the number of people with a self-employed lifestyle can be expected to be less in urban areas than in rural areas where the number of self-employed has traditionally been higher, amongst other things because of small independent family farms. As these have been amalgamated, a significant part of the workforce that was exposed to the self-employed lifestyle during childhood has been forced to find alternative possibilities of existence. These people will be motivated to establish themselves as self-employed if they can. With this foundation, a greater desire to be an entrepreneur can be assumed in rural areas and among people from rural areas who for various reasons have been forced to settle in urban areas.

Looking at job developments in Denmark since the beginning of the 1970s, a clear fall has occurred in the number of jobs in manufacturing industry in the Greater Copenhagen area at the same time as growth in the number of people employed in the private and public service sectors. As far as developments in the number of new jobs in manufacturing industry are concerned, these have mostly taken place in the provinces, especially in Jutland.[3]

There is a particularly high concentration of entrepreneurs in manufacturing industry in Jutland and a growth in the number of jobs in this sector. There are many reasons for this, as Bue Nielsen, amongst others has pointed out.[4] One factor he did not include was the local tradition for independent employment. In a comparative analysis of business development in the area of Ikast, Jutland and on the south-eastern islands Lolland-Falster, Hjalager expresses the opinion that the fact that a relatively large part of the population in the Ikast area grew up in homes where the parents had been independent caused greater dynamism in entrepreneurial activities than on Lolland-Falster, where the number of self-employed has always been lower.[5] In a report from the Ministry of the Environment "Danmarks Byregioner" from 1992, it is stressed that the cultural character and lifestyle which typifies western Denmark and small town communities is of significance for entrepreneurial activity. "The strong trades and agricultural traditions have contributed to great initiative and flexibility...more tradesmen and industrial businesses are started in these areas than in those dominated by the wage-earner lifestyle."[6]

The number of jobs in industry in the region round the capital has fallen by a third in the past 20 years. The recession in industry has been especially severe in Copenhagen itself. There is a lack of people with vitality and the get-up-and-go mentality. A large part of the workforce has traditionally comprised people with an "earner" lifestyle, both the wage-earner lifestyle and the careerist lifestyle. People with the self-employed lifestyle have been under-represented but in the past significant numbers of people migrated from the provinces to the city. For a long time Copenhagen had a monopoly of higher education, and young people seeking higher education had to look for it in Copenhagen, where many of them put down roots and established their own companies. In recent decades, decentralisation of higher education has taken place, and technological developments in methods of communication have meant that entrepreneurs no longer have to move to Copenhagen.

As a substitute for the vital Danes from the provinces streaming to the area, Copenhagen today is in the fortunate situation of having received a significant number of the immigrants and refugees who have come to Denmark. Many arrive with a self-employed background and the entrepreneurial desire that native inhabitants of Copenhagen lack, and in recent years a strong growth has occurred, with many of the new ethnic minorities setting themselves up in business.

In 1980, 13.86% of the Danish population who were active in the labour market were self-employed. This figure had fallen to 10.06% in 1994. In comparison it can be mentioned that in 1990, 6.77% of the Turkish inhabitants, 2.59% of the immigrants from Yugoslavia and 20.58% of the Pakistani inhabitants were self-employed. This figure had risen in 1994 to 14.13% for Turkish inhabitants, 3.53% for the immigrants from the former Yugoslavia, and 31.49% for Pakistani inhabitants.[7] The increase in the number of self-employed among immigrants from Pakistan and Turkey was rapid, and this figure may not even reveal the true picture. There are grounds for believing that if the many Pakistani immigrants who have become Danish citizens were taken into account, the proportion of independent self-employed among people of Pakistani origin would be higher than the 31.49% (see Figure 12).

Before emigrating from their homeland, many immigrants had their roots in a self-employed lifestyle, and if they become unemployed and can-not fulfil their dream of saving up to return home and establish themselves as self-employed, they will try to establish themselves as self-employed in the country to which they have immigrated. It can therefore be expected that immigrants with a rural background will break out of passive existence as unemployed and try to establish themselves as self-employed.[8]

Self-employed people are not subject to the same price for labour which applies to collective agreements. Self-employed people decide for themselves how much they will have for their work. It is therefore possible to establish oneself as self-employed, but it is often under much more difficult working conditions and with the investment of longer working hours that such businesses get by in competition with larger concerns with plenty of capital behind them.

It is primarily in commerce and service that establishment as self-employed by immigrants and refugees takes place, mostly small shops, restaurants, taxis and cleaning firms. Apart from taxis, they are very largely family businesses, which get by under difficult working conditions and extremely long working-hours. I do not agree with Schierup when he says that, "Families who 'strike out on their own' do not do it because they are especially 'business-minded'"[9] while I am more in agreement with him when he completes the sentence, "but because private concerns can, at best, form a source of a certain economic security, provided the family is prepared to accept a low standard of living".[10]

In my opinion, many immigrants are especially business-minded. A very large number of them originally came to work and save up to return home and establish themselves as self-employed. The majority of Pakistani and Turkish immigrants grew up in self-employed households, and their goal in life when they emigrated was to be free and independently self-employed themselves. For various reasons, which I have explained elsewhere,[11] it was not possible for them to realise this dream. In recognising that the possibilities for returning home were no longer open and that it is difficult to get a job, more and more choose to realise their dream of a life in self-employment in Denmark. Many of them are, therefore, especially business-minded, and it is characteristic that those who have their roots in a wage-earner lifestyle do not establish themselves as self-employed to any great extent. This is true, for instance, of immigrants from former Yugoslavia, who do not have a background as self-employed in their homeland to the same extent as immigrants from Pakistan and Turkey. Many were wage-earners and worked as smiths, mechanics or welders before coming to Denmark. Their goal in life was not primarily an existence as independent self-employed as, for instance, for many immigrants from Turkey and Pakistan.

By establishing themselves as independently self-employed in Copenhagen and some other urban areas, immigrants and refugees are currently on the way to establishing a low-pay area (if their effort is measured against hourly earnings) for the production of service functions.[12]

There are both advantages and disadvantages connected with the development of low-paid independent family concerns. The first disadvantage is that the price of labour in this sector is low measured per hour, but, for people with the self-employed lifestyle, the amount earned per hour is not as important as being live as free and independent businessmen. This is the goal of people with a self-employed lifestyle, and the children and young people who grow up in this environment will to a large extent be influenced by the energy which characterises people with this lifestyle, and they exist in the hope that their economic situation will improve. Immigrants are thus an important contributory force in the development of a "Global City", with their many ethnic restaurants, their activities in the transport sector, and their efforts to keep everything clean and tidy, contributing to colleagues in industrial services being interested in using Copenhagen as an international base. Copenhagen should count itself lucky that it has received a much-needed blood transfusion in the form of energetic and enterprising refugees and immigrants.

The informal economy

In 1987, Portes and Sassen-Koob published the theory that developments in post-industrial society would lead to the formation of an informal economy, with very low pay for the labour force.[13] They rightly reject the many theories, which assert that informal economies are especially a characteristic of the third world, where they are thought to be a refuge from want and misery, and which will disappear as modern industrial production arises. They claim that in connection with the development of a post-industrial society, an informal economy will arise especially carried out by small independent firms. This claim is not necessarily correct. People performing "black" labour may well be employed in large industrial or service companies, from which they earn their main income. The "black" labour is performed in their free time and the income is regarded as a supplement to their main income; "black" labour can be performed by people with all types of lifestyle. Investigations in Denmark show, for instance, that much of the "black" work is carried out by skilled tradesmen with legal jobs.[14]

In order to understand the informal sector, it is first necessary to reveal what the demand is for "black" labour, what form of qualifications are necessary, and to what degree it is true that "black" labour is a supplement to the workers' normal income or whether it is something that the individual lives by totally and completely. Only in cases where an individual must live by "black" labour can the person concerned be forced to work for extremely low pay.

Portes and Sassen-Koob mention that it could be a case of pre-capitalist production modes, without explaining precisely what they mean. They do not make it clear that in and by the establishment of small independent firms, whether operated partially or wholly in the "white" economic sector, the capitalist production mode is in many cases abandoned and people are confronted with the simple commodity production mode which has quite other requirements to living conditions than those I have described for the capitalist production mode.[15]

Even though Marx, Weber and other theorists predicted that small independent firms would disappear as the concentration of capital increases,[16] this prediction has not been fulfilled. Whether it will is an open question.[17] Small, independent, family-based firms have shown themselves in certain circumstances to be very resistant to fluctuation. Such manufacturing units can function for long periods without any actual return from the operational resources in relation to the normal levels of interest and rates of profit in concerns run on a capitalist basis. By supplementing with income from a subsidiary occupation, reducing profits or increasing production, small independent firms can survive periods of falling prices where real capital would be withdrawn from the particular production and placed in other sectors. This means that where large-scale operations requiring a high level of finance do not offset this difference, the capitalist production mode will not be able to out-compete the simple commodity production in the long run. A possible economic subordination of this, if it exists, will instead be of an indirect kind, for instance through the manufacturer's dependence on borrowed, interest-bearing capital.

The idea that technological development will always promote large-scale operations is not necessarily correct. In certain cases the development of new technology removes the former established advantages of large-scale operations and opens up the possibility for simple commodity producers to continue or increase their share. For instance, Danish industry builds to a large extent on small and medium-sized companies, where new technology has often removed the former advantages of large-scale operations and made smaller companies more competitive. Højrup[18] has looked at developments in the transport sector, where a number of small and medium-sized transport companies have arisen which have had favourable conditions because of State investment in the road system so that the producers themselves only need to invest in rolling stock.

Simple commodity producers do not necessarily have to be small companies. Theoretically, one can imagine companies with several hundred employees. These are companies where the firm's economy and the owner's private economy are one and the same and where, in times of difficulty, the owner does not sell the company and invest the capital released in other companies or securities with a better return.

The desire to avoid taxation by not declaring all income forms the basis for an informal economy. In countries where employers are obliged to pay significant amounts in social insurance for their employees in addition to paying tax for their employees, there is a motivation for developing special ways to avoid paying the tax.

In order to avoid paying tax and social security, employers in certain countries let their employees register as independently self-employed, because as independently self-employed they are personally responsible for paying social security contributions if they wish to be insured. If these "self-employed" people are willing to work for less than the minimum rate of pay for a worker, the employer receives an economic benefit. Another method is to let labourers from another EU country or from a land outside the EU retain their residence in their homeland, so that if necessary they pay tax and social security contributions in their homeland. If this is a country with low levels of pay and low taxation, it is possible to get such labourers to work for less than the normal rates of pay. Finally, in certain countries, there are rules that mandatory social security contributions need not be paid for people in part-time employment or for persons working in agriculture. To avoid the mandatory social security payments, various atypical types of employment conditions can be expected to occur.

In Denmark, the informal economy has been the subject of systematic research since 1980.[19] Comprehensive surveys have been carried out at intervals of two to four years in an unbroken sequence since 1980, the latest having been conducted in November 1994. Besides these surveys, others have studied the informal economy from its effect on cash-flow and differences in declared income and the gross national product.[20]

Figure 9:   Trends in the "informal economy"

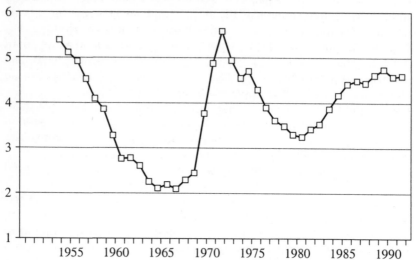

Source: Filip Sundram, Specialopgave 1995, kenemisk Institut v. KU.

The role of the informal economy in the total economy of Denmark has fluctuated. A recent study by Filip Sundram focuses on the extent of the informal economy compared with the Danish GNP from 1953 to 1991.[21] The figures show that the informal economy comprised 5.4% of the GNP in 1953. From 1953 to 1966 it decreased, then it started to increase again, reaching a peak in 1972. After 1972, it decreased until 1980, when a new increase started, peaking in 1991.

Sundram explains these fluctuations by referring to developments on the Danish labour market. According to Sundram, the high level of the informal economy at the start of the 1950s was related to the fact that agriculture was still the main sector in the economy, and that local authorities at that time accepted that small farmers helped each other during the harvest and so on, without being taxed on the value of the work done for each other. Also within the domestic sector, there were many "black" activities at the time. Many middle-class households employed people to do cleaning and other household duties without informing the tax authorities.

From 1953 on, Denmark changed from being an agricultural society to an industrial one. The traditional opportunities for "black" work were reduced at the same time as taxable employment in the industrial sector increased. In 1965, the informal economy only comprised 2% of the GNP.

The economic boom in the late 1950s and early 1960s resulted in a building boom in private housing. In the middle 1960s, taxes rose. More and more houses were privately built, resulting in a sharp increase in "black" labour. There was an explosive growth in the informal economy in 1971. In the following years, the situation changed. Methods of taxation improved and more and more Danes became "do-it-yourself" people, reducing the need for "black" labour. The informal economy decreased from 5.6% of the GNP in 1971 to 3.2% in 1980. Due to inflation and wage increases in the late 1970s, the financial situation of many private house-owners improved, resulting in a lot of rebuilding activity in the 1980s. In the same period, there was a constant increase in taxation, and many chose to have work on their houses and so on carried out by "black" labour. This created a new boom in the informal economy, which reached a peak at 4.7% of the GNP in 1991.

Surveys carried out from 1980 and onwards have given us detailed information about many sides of "black" activities in Denmark.[22] Table 8 shows the types of "black" activities from 1988/89 to 1994. Around 30% of the activities are related to building, largely in connection with home improvements such as painting, joinery and bricklaying, and about 10% on repair work on cars, household durable goods, etc. "Black" labour in housework, child-minding, etc., is very limited.

Most of the "black" activities are carried out by young men, who are often skilled workers.[23] Regionally, the highest rate for "black" activity is West Jutland, where 27.8% of the respondents participated in "black" work compared with only 8.7% in Copenhagen. "Black" labour is usually recruited from the close social network of the employer, and immigrants usually have neither the skills nor the social contacts necessary for such employment.[24] Furthermore, "black" work is most widespread in regions with low concentration of immigrants and refugees.

The structure of the labour market in Denmark and the other Nordic countries is different from the rest of the EU States. The activity rate among women is very high, a prerequisite for this being a high level of kindergartens, crèches and other day-care facilities for children. The demand for domestic servants is extremely low, which reduces employment opportunities for illegal immigrants in this sector. In Berlin, I have been told, it is quite common for Polish teachers and others who can speak German to be employed in cleaning work in middle-class German households at weekends. No such situation exists in Denmark.

Table 8: Types of "black" activities 1988/89-1994

	1988	1991	1993	1994
Agriculture, forestry and fishing (DB93: 01.00.00-05.03.00)	13.6	20.3	11.2	14.3
(e.g. gardening, agricultural and animal husbandry service, chopping wood, sale of pigs, catching fish for sale from own boat)				
Manufacturing (DB93: 15.00.00-37.20.00)	5.6	4.2	5.0	5.6
(e.g. production etc. of meat and meat products, sewing, maintenance and repair of boats)				
Building and construction (DB93: 45.00.00-45.50.00)	28.7	22.8	33.0	28.7
- bricklaying	3.1	2.1	2.8	2.5
- paving	0.6	0.8	1.7	1.6
- electrical work	2.6	1.7	3.4	5.3
- plumbing	2.1	0.8	1.7	1.2
- joinery installation	5.1	4.1	5.0	5.0
- carpentry and decoration	1.8	2.1	1.1	0.9
- painting and glazing	4.0	0.8	7.8	4.0
- other (e.g. "built a house", "helped friend")	9.4	10.4	9.5	8.2
Trade and repair work (DB93: 50.00.00-52.74.90)	13.2	12.9	11.1	10.0
- maintenance and repair of cars	7.2	5.4	5.6	5.3
- other (e.g. retail sail and repair of personal and household goods, welding)	6.0	7.5	5.5	4.7
Hotel and restaurants etc. (DB93: 55.00.00-55.52.00)	6.2	7.8	8.4	6.5
(e.g. cooking and serving food)				
Transport (DB93: 60.00.00-64.20.00)	3.5	4.2	6.7	5.9
- business related service etc. (DB93: 70.00.00-74.84.90)	13.1	9.1	10.1	11.8
- accounting, book-keeping, auditing etc.	2.9	1.7	1.7	2.5
- cleaning	5.3	4.6	5.0	3.7
- other (e.g. legal and computer activities)	4.9	2.8	3.4	5.6
Education (DB93: 80.00.00-80.42.90)	0.6	1.7	0.6	0.6
Medical activities, social institutions etc. (DB93: 85.00.00-85.32.90)	5.4	6.6	5.1	5.9
- looking after children	4.5	4.6	3.9	3.4
- other (e.g. zone therapy, home care)	0.9	2.0	1.2	2.5
Organisations, recreational, cultural and sporting activities, other service activities (DB93: 90.00.00-95.00.00)	6.9	7.9	6.1	6.5
(e.g. composing songs and music, musicians, sports training, hairdressing)				
Activity not stated (DB93: 98.00.00)	3.2	2.5	2.8	4.0
Total	100.0	100.0	100.1	99.8

Source: Viby-Mogensen: The Shadow Economy in Denmark 1994 Measurement and Results.
Note: Totals may not be exactly 100% because of rounding of figures. The black activities are coded according to the Danish Industrial Classification of Economic Activities 1993: DB93/NACE.

The way in which the informal economy is organised and has developed in Denmark does not indicate any special market for "black" labour with wage rates at extremely low levels as we know from other countries, for instance migrant farm workers in the USA.

At the turn of the century, Denmark had unemployment problems in agriculture and many farm workers emigrated to the USA, Canada or Australia. At the same time, Denmark imported Polish labour to work in the sugar beet fields.[25] These Polish workers were paid less than an unemployed Danish farm worker would accept, and a special market for extremely low-paid labour was established. These Poles were not illegal immigrants. Before 1926, few restrictions were imposed on foreigners who wanted to live and work in Denmark, but a law was then passed requiring foreigners to obtain a labour permits.[26] Such permits could only be issued if in the opinion of the authorities it was in the national interest. In practice it meant that foreigners could only get a labour permit if qualified Danish labour was not available. So an extremely low-paid labour market for unskilled immigrants was not established.

Because of allowances for materials, pay, etc., in the ordinary economy, firms are suppliers rather than purchasers in the informal economy. They therefore have but little interest in purchasing illegal immigrant labour. Very few of the people working in the informal economy in Denmark have "black" labour as their most important or only form of income. The majority involved in "black" activities have a normal job and only work the "black" labour market to supplement their income. The expression "the "black" labour market" is therefore somewhat misleading here, since a market creates contact between random suppliers and purchasers. This is not the case in Denmark, where "black" labour is performed within narrow social groups consisting of families, friends and colleagues. Wages on the "black" labour market often correspond to the saving made by not declaring income to the tax authorities.

Notes

1   Qvortrup 1993: 2.
2   There can also be economic problems, but the fact that one may not, for instance, study for further qualifications while receiving unemployment benefit may be considered unfair.
3   B. Nielsen 1995; Arbejdspladsprognose 1991-2010 for kommuner og amter i hovedstadsregionen; Maskell 1994, Illeris 1990; Ministry of the Environment 1992.
4   B. Nielsen 1995.
5   Hjalager.
6   Ministry of the Environment 1992: 56.
7   Schierup 1993: 108.
8   Schierup 1993: 109.
9   Schierup 1993: 109.
10 Schierup 1993: 109.
11 Hjarnø 1971, 1991.

12 Note the Danish authorities have revealed that a lot of "black" work is carried out by some immigrants and that some exploit the possibility of getting an enterprise allowance to qualify for unemployment benefit. No figures have been published as to the extent.

13 Portes & Sassen-Koob 1987.

14 Viby-Mogensen 1994.

15 Depending on taxation, effectivity of tax assessment, etc.

16 Marx 1964: 1064; Weber 1905; Lipset & Rokkan 1967; Vidich & Bensman 1960.

17 The elements in a production mode are not connected with simple causes/effects, but on the contrary with complex structures which represent a kind of mutual cause and effect relationship. Godelier pointed out in 1966 (Godelier 1966) that it was important to distinguish between intersystemic and intrasystemic conflicts. In the framework of the capitalist production mode, there is an intrasystemic conflict between capital and labour, whilst intersystemic conflicts are conflicts between differing production modes, between different structures. In the analysis of capitalism, the intrasystemic conflict relationship (the class struggle) is insufficient in itself to cause a breakdown in the system. The better the working class is at organising itself, the greater the share of the profits it will receive. At the same time, it must not go so far that the capital does not make a good profit, or the businesses will close. Between production modes, therefore, there is intersystemic conflict, a competition that can result in one production mode dominating another and possibly totally out-competing it so that it disappears. Competition on the global level currently stands primarily between the capitalist mode of production and the simple commodity and service mode of production, and nobody at the present time can predict whether the latter will out-compete the former or whether a whole new production mode will arise. Modern technological developments have done away with the advantages of large-scale operations in many areas. As to what the consequences may be, Manuel Castells, amongst others, has considered in his book "The Informational City", at which it will unfortunately be out of place to look more closely here (see Castells 1989).

18 Højrup 1995.

19   Dahlgaard 1983; Viby-Mogensen 1985a, 1985b, 1987, 1989, 1990a, 1990b, 1992; Viby-Mogensen, Kvist, Körmendi & Pedersen 1995.
20   Jepsen 1994; Sundram 1995.
21   Sundram 1995.
22   Viby-Mogensen 1990; Viby-Mogensen, Kvist, Körmendi & Petersen 1995: 26-27.
23   Viby-Mogensen, Kvist, Körmendi & Petersen 1995: 27-29.
24   Viby-Mogensen 1990: 45-50.
25   Nelleman 1981.
26   Law no. 80 of 31st March 1926.

6 The Effect of Organising

The organisation of labour markets in the EU

The most notable differences between developments in the USA and in Denmark result from the way in which their labour markets are organised, though the way in which they and the State interact is different.[1] In Denmark, the trade union movement and the employers' organisations have developed a civilised, well-functioning democratic collaboration in the labour market, while conditions in America are largely controlled by the employers, because the trade union movement is weak and unable to mobilise counter-measures.

In the EU, too, there are major differences between countries in the way the labour market is organised.[2] In the Nordic countries, Great Britain and Germany, there are united trade union movements divided into trades, while a number of countries in Central and Southern Europe have different unions for Christians and non-Christians, Communists, Socialists and others. It must be assumed that a united movement is stronger that one divided into branches with ideological differences.

There are also major differences in the rate of organisation amongst employees across the EU.[3] In the Nordic countries the rate among employees is 80-90%, the highest in the EU.[4] Apart from Belgium, none of the other EU countries have rates of organisation above 50% and several, especially in Southern Europe, are down around 10-15%.[5] These rates partially reflect the power of the trade union movements, the strongest and most powerful trade unions, measured in terms of membership, being the Nordic ones.

The classic conflict between capital and labour in the Nordic countries brought about the organisation of workers into trade unions and employers into employers' associations. About 100 years ago, the conflict between capital and labour caused serious and devastating conflicts in the Scandinavian countries. These ended when the two sides signed a truce under which employers recognised the right of workers to organise themselves into trade unions and the unions' right to negotiate pay and conditions on behalf of their members, while the employees and trade unions recognised the employers' right to direct and allocate work.[6] The first truces, or main agreements, were established in Denmark in 1899, in Sweden in 1906, and in Norway in 1907.[7]

Employers have the right to make decisions on a number of questions concerning employment and occupation. For instance they may enter into employment contracts, make promotions and demotions, direct and allocate work, check performance, take disciplinary measures, dismiss workers, etc. Up to 1995 employers' prerogatives also included the right to discriminate on the grounds of race[8] and it still include the right to negotiate individual conditions of employment at will, as well as freedom from control by the civil courts. Disputes are settled in the Industrial Court, which comprises representatives from the organisations and a civil judge. The right to direct and allocate work constitutes the fundamental rule in most Nordic labour legislation.

In line with the traditional Nordic emphasis on collective agreements and labour market organisation, the most important regulation has been the system of collective bargaining and grievance procedures, while protection of the individual's employment is weak. When a collective agreement is reached, normally every other year, it is the responsibility of the employers' associations and the trade unions to keep the peace.[9]

The embargo on strikes and lock-outs is comprehensive in the Nordic countries and Germany, but no such embargo exists in Great Britain or France. According to Nielsen,[10] the powerful embargo on strikes and lock-outs implies that the right to strike is not an individual civil right, but a collective one administered by the trade unions on behalf of the workers. In France, the right to strike is regarded as an individual civil right and is protected under the Constitution. The decision to strike lies with the individual and not with an organisation, and the Danish rules on keeping the peace would probably be an infringement of the French Constitution. In Italy, Greece, Spain, Luxembourg and Portugal, the right to strike is guaranteed under their constitutions, and indirectly also in Germany, Holland and Belgium. In Great Britain and Ireland, there is no specific legislation on this point.

Lock-outs are forbidden under the Constitution in Portugal, and by law in Greece. In France, Italy and Germany, lock-outs are allowed under certain circumstances. In Spain and Luxembourg lock-outs are legal, and in Belgium they are a tolerated weapon. In Great Britain, Ireland and the Nordic countries, lock-outs are regarded as an acceptable counter-measure to strikes, while in Holland the legal situation is obscure.

Scandinavia is unique in an international context in having collective agreements accepting the employers' right to direct and allocate work and the workers' right to organise. In Britain, Germany, France, the USA and a number of other countries, the trade unions have never recognised the right of the employers to direct and allocate work but have continued to maintain a more militant line of confrontation.[11] Summers is certainly correct when he says that the lack of recognition of the employers' right to direct and allocate work has resulted in the trade union movement outside Scandinavia never having attained the size and importance that it has there.[12]

The tenor of Danish, and Scandinavian, labour law is collective labour legislation with collective agreements, and case law from the Industrial Courts as the main source of law. The Constitution plays only a minor role in labour legislation in the Nordic countries.[13] The fundamental rights of industrial law, individual as well as collective, are less protected in the Nordic countries than in most EU States, especially at Constitutional level.[14]

Compared with other EU countries, Nordic employers enjoy an exceptionally high degree of freedom in individual conditions of employment, a fact that often surprises foreigners, who expect that countries with strong trade union movements and an elaborate welfare system should protect the individual employee to a degree that, at least, corresponds to the average European standard. According to Nielsen,[15] one of the reasons for this apparent inconsistency is the widespread view in the Nordic Social Democratic parties and the trade union movement that social protection should be derived not from the employer but from collective agreements and the welfare state, enabling employees to remain more independent of their employers than under a system with stronger emphasis on individual employment protection, which could result in identification between employees and employers.

Most Nordic welfare state legislation dates back to the period between the 1930s and the 1970s. This applies, for example, to legislation on unemployment and sickness benefit, holidays, maternity leave, etc. This form of legislation primarily gives rights to the individual employee in relation to the State, and not normally in relation to the employer. Large portions of the Nordic social security and social welfare system are financed through taxation and are not closely linked to paid employment. The political force behind the creation of the Nordic welfare state was the Social Democratic parties, which are now, as always, closely linked to the trade union movement.

Illegal immigrants

Under the Nordic system, the two sides of the labour market recognise each other as partners, both having the right to arm themselves. And armed they are. The trade unions have built up huge strike funds, and in the event of a conflict they can order their members who are still at work to make extraordinary contributions to allow their striking colleagues to be paid an amount which ensures that they can largely maintain their former standard of living. Similarly, the employers' associations have built up funds so as to redress the losses of members who are enforcing a lock-out or who are hit by a blockade. Under this system, both parties recognise the power of the other. Both know that if it comes to open conflict, it can have devastating consequences, not only for the contending parties but also for society as a whole. It is therefore of overwhelming importance for both parties to maintain a truce, which demands that both sides adhere to collective agreements. This has created a high degree of responsibility among both workers and employers. Employers who do not respect the agreement will quickly be threatened by the trade union movement, as well as by their own association.

In normal circumstances, the State does not need to interfere, since the employers' association has a primary interest in not breaking agreements with the trade union movement and will not accept individual employers breaking the agreements and threatening the truce between capital and labour. Employing illegal labour immigrants is not acceptable, and Danish employers are therefore reluctant to take them on.

In Denmark there is freedom of organisation; no employer is obliged to be a member of an employers association and the same freedom applies to employees: No-one is forced to be a member of a trade union in order to take employment.[16] However, there are exceptions. Some companies who are not members of an employers' association, have signed local agreements with the unions containing a clause compelling the company to employ only organised labour.[17] In many cases it is difficult for employers not to be organised. If they do not follow the collective agreements regarding pay and working conditions, they can expect to be brought into line by strikes or blockades.

In 1969 and 1970, the number of foreigners looking for work in Denmark rose drastically.[18] At that time a number of companies established in the boom years were not organised under the Danish Federation of Employers. Some of their owners tried to pay foreign workers wages below the collective rates,[19] despite the fact that workers all had labour permits which demanded they be paid according to the collective agreements.[20] Immigrants at that time were not organised and did not know the ordinary rates, and were therefore quite happy with the pay they received. It was a difficult situation, because very few Danes could communicate with the immigrants and ask for copies of their pay-slips, which would have made it possible for the unions to check on whether they were being paid in accordance with collective agreements. At that time I was organising cultural and social associations for various nationalities of labour immigrants, and in that connection I received financial support from the Danish Federation of Employers as well as from the Danish General Workers Union and the Hotel and Restaurant Workers Union. At association meetings, I had no difficulty in getting immigrants to bring their pay-slips so that I could take copies for the unions. Where immigrants were underpaid, the local unions used these pay-slips as documentation to force unorganised employers to pay in accordance with the rules. The reason for the economic support I received from the Danish Federation of Employers was stated to be a measure to maintain peace and prevent the development of negative attitudes towards foreign employees who had agreed to work for pay below the ordinary rates. Within a few months, the underpayment of labour migrants had ceased, and many of the unorganised employers had joined an employers' association.

Although there is freedom of organisation in Denmark in general, there was one exception until 1995. Foreign nationals granted labour permits were obliged to join an unemployment insurance scheme for the first two years. Since these schemes are managed by the local trade unions, the foreigners usually also join the union, which has resulted in a higher rate of union membership among legal immigrants in Denmark than in other countries.[21]

The Scandinavian system of mutual collaboration between employers and employees exercises a social control which up to now has been very effective in keeping illegal labour migrants out, and in normal circumstances the State has no need to interfere. The sanctions, which can be used against employers who try to employ illegal immigrants, are used comparatively rarely.

In EU States with no similar strong system of collective agreements controlling relations between employers and employees, the State plays a much more active role in the labour market. Here, the risks involved in breaking the law by employing illegal immigrants depend on the resources mobilized by the State for direct control of individual employees through inspection and the severity of the sanctions enforced against them. I have not yet studied this system in any non-Scandinavian country, but I expect to find that the less risk there is of being caught employing illegal immigrants and the less severe the punishment is for breaking the law, the more inclined employers will be to employ illegal immigrants, provided there is a need for the qualifications which they can offer.

According to "Migration News",[22] Germany probably spends more on preventing the employment of illegal labour immigrants than any other country. In 1994, there were over 78,000 inspections of German employers suspected of employing illegal aliens. Almost half (42,000) led to fines and warnings. Germany has about 1,500 industrial inspectors, at an annual cost of around DM 100,000 per inspector. The Ministry of Labour spends about DM 150 million annually in preventing German workers from drawing unemployment insurance benefit while working and in checking work-places for illegal immigrants.

"Migration News" also states that German officials believe that the desire to preserve a generous welfare state and an orderly labour market gives them the resources necessary for effective enforcement. For example, German inspectors can obtain local police support for work-site inspections at no cost to the Ministry of Labour. When four or five inspectors enter a construction site, for instance, they may have 50 or 100 local police surrounding the site to prevent workers from escaping. German officials report that German companies try to avoid negative publicity and therefore prefer to pay fines rather than contest them in court. If a German company contests a fine, its name can become public. Fines contested in court are registered with the local Chamber of Commerce, and public agencies and other companies can require employers tendering for con-tracts to provide information on the firm's violations of labour laws and regulations.

A sweep of hotels and restaurants involving 3,600 inspectors and police in March 1995 found that 830 of the restaurants inspected employed illegal aliens.

My immediate reaction to the above was a mental picture of a police state. Nothing like this normally happens in Denmark.[23] I only know of few cases where Danish employers have taken on illegal immigrants. Most of them involve Polish "tourists" working illegally for small employers on berry-picking and other seasonal activities. Another case involved a Danish boat-builder of Polish origin that employed some Polish "tourists" illegally. Finally, there was a case in the press in which a Danish employer had employed a team of Polish "tourists" illegally in connection with the renovation of a house. In all these cases, the employer was not organised in the employers' association and the breach of the law was stopped immedi-ately. According to the police, these cases do not represent the tip of an iceberg; there is not a lot of illegal labour immigration under the surface.[24]

Summary

The organisation of the labour market and the interplay between the parties in the labour market and the State play a decisive role for the existence of illegal immigrants in the labour market. In a society with well-developed, civilised, democratic collaboration between the trade unions and the employers, where both sides have mutually recognised the other's rights and duties, the collaboration creates a mutual social control which counteracts employers taking on illegal labour immigrants. There is no need for State control of the workplace.

In societies where the trade union movement is weak and close democratic collaboration between employers and employees does not exist, it remains up to the State to ensure that employers do not take on illegal labour immigrants. Such control craves many resources, and the presence of large numbers of illegal immigrants in the majority of EU States outside Scandinavia bears witness that State control is inadequate.

Notes

1 J. R. Commons and others, *History of Labor in the United States*, New York, 1921-35 (4 vols.); J. G. Rayback, *A History of American Labor*, New York, 1966.
2 SEC (89) 1137, 7 et seq.
3 SEC (89) 1137, 7 ff.
4 Scheuer has just published a detailed investigation on the spread of collective bargaining and trade union organisation in Denmark. His results question the myth of the very high rate. In smaller firms in the private sector with from 1 to 10 employees, only 35% are covered by a collective agreement, while in large companies with more than 1,000 employees the corresponding figure is 81%. A total of 52% of employees in the private sector were covered by a collective agreement in 1994, but this figure varied between 65% in the foodstuff industry to only 31% in shops and commerce.

   The rate for the total private sector is between 46.4% and 53.5%, depending on the method of calculation, and the corresponding figure for the total labour market is 65% to 70%. This is pioneering work where it is difficult to draw definite conclusions on developments in the rates (Scheuer 1996).

5   Traxler 1994, chap. 5.
6   Bruun 1938; Due, Madsen & Jensen 1993.
7   Bruun 1938, Nielsen 1992, Due, Madsen & Jensen 1993.
8   The Danish Parliament (the Folketing) is currently discussing a Bill which, if accepted, will make it illegal to discriminate on the basis of race, ethnic origin or national descent.
9   Nielsen 1992: 71-191; Illum 1964: 244 ff; Jacobsen 1987: chap. VIII.
10   Nielsen 1992: 110.
11   Nielsen 1992: 177-178. Trade unions in Great Britain no longer take a militant line of confrontation. They were forced onto the defensive in the 1980s and have now in many cases altered their policies towards a significantly more "integrated" form of bargaining (Beaumont 1995).
12   Summers 1983: 589 ff.
13   R. Nielsen 1995.
14   Nielsen 1992.
15   R. Nielsen 1995.
16   Nielsen 1992.
17   Nielsen 1992: 76-78; Jacobsen 1974: 293 ff; Illum 1964: 187; Rise 1983: 196 ff.
18   Hjarnø 1995.
19   DASF 1970.
20   Hjarnø 1995. Labour permits could only be issued if payment was made in accordance with the local agreements or according to what was customary.
21   Act. No. 114 of 24th March, 1970; Order No. 238 of 2nd May 1973.
22   Migration News, Vol. 2, No. 8, August 1995.
23   However, in February 1996, Danish television broadcast a programme in which officials from Customs and Excise, together with the police, made a sweep of pizza houses. It showed, for instance, a "brother" who was "just visiting from Turkey", who was caught with pizza dough on his fingers. It appeared that this had also occurred during a previous sweep. I have asked the police for an account of similar cases and have been advised that they are extremely rare, and that statistics are not kept on them.
24   Here I am only taking into consideration work carried out by foreign nationals without a labour permit. I am well aware that illegal activities go on in connection with people carrying out black labour

and receiving unemployment benefits at the same time. This is social fraud, which is not the subject of this work.

7 Trends in Portugal, Germany and Denmark

Developments in Portugal

As an example of an EU country with low pay levels, weak trade unions and an under-developed social welfare system, and which imports labour, we shall look at conditions in Portugal.

After the revolution in 1974, which led to the opening up of the economy, Portugal has been an under-developed country compared with most of the rest of Western Europe. It has become increasingly open to the rest of the world, and nationalised concerns have been privatised. This, in combination with the stable political situation, has attracted private capital for the establishment of new companies in the manufacturing sector. Since Portugal's entry into the EU on January 1st, 1986, significant grants from the large structural funds in the EU towards construction and the infrastructure have contributed to an acceleration of the internationalisation of the economy.[1] Since the end of the 1980s, this has led to a reduction in unemployment[2] and a shortage of labour in certain sectors.

In the 1960s, Portugal was a major supplier of foreign labour to a number of countries in Western Europe, amongst others to France, Germany and Switzerland,[3] and at the end of the 1960s this migration, combined with a growing need for soldiers for the escalating wars in the Portuguese colonies, caused a lack of unskilled labour, amongst other places in the construction industry, which they tried to solve by importing Africans from the colonies.[4] The importation of foreign labour can thus be traced back to the late 1960s (see Figure 10).

The 1974 revolution and the subsequent de-colonization resulted in a growth in immigration from the former African colonies, partly of people of Portuguese origin and partly of Africans. This immigration was only partially due to lack of labour in Portugal, since the majority came for political reasons.

Figure 10: Foreign nationals in Portugal

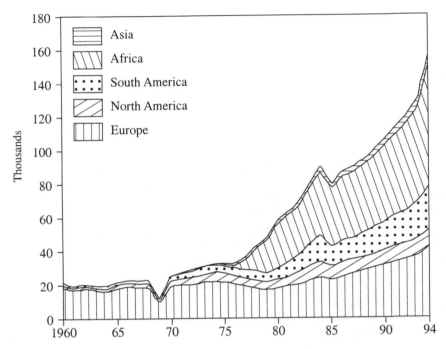

Source: Maria Beatriz Rocha-Trindade, Portugal: The New Framework of Migration Policies (1993).

At the same time as this immigration, part of which took place illegally, there was also emigration of Portuguese nationals. Since Portugal's entry into the EU in January 1986, it has been possible for Portuguese to take employment freely in the other EU States, without having to apply for a labour permit. Many unskilled workers took jobs in the construction industry in Germany. There has, moreover, been a migration of labour to other countries in Europe (for instance Switzerland), America and South Africa.[5] Portugal's importation of unskilled labour from the former African colonies during recent years is thus mainly thought to be a substitute for Portuguese nationals who have emigrated.[6]

In connection with accession to the Schengen agreement, Portugal passed new legislation regarding the issuing of residence and labour permits. To obtain a labour permit, citizens from outside the EU must obtain a residence and labour permit before travelling to Portugal. The applicant must have a letter of employment from an employer. The application must be approved by the Labour Inspectorate and approval is only given if local workers able to carry out the work cannot be found. In firms with more than five employees, 90% of the people employed must be Portuguese citizens.[7]

The armed conflicts in the former colonies of Angola and Mozambique resulted in further waves of immigration. At the start of the 1980s, a lack of available labour began to form the background for increased immigration of Chinese, Pakistanis, Indians and Africans from the former Portuguese colonies and from South America, particularly from Brazil. Immigration of people from countries outside the EU is still taking place, about 1.3% of the total population in 1993 being foreign nationals.[8]

Table 9 shows changes in the number of foreign nationals employed during the period 1983-1994, classified by trade. The figures clearly reflect the demand for labour, which has partly been a need for highly qualified workers (engineers, designers, marketing people and managers) and partly unskilled labourers in industry, construction and in private households. During the period 1983-1994, the group of experts and technicians rose by 354.3% from 4,082 to 18,543. The figures also show that in terms of percentages, the growth in the number of foreign nationals was especially high for the first three groups between 1983 and 1990, whilst growth in domestic service was noticeable from 1990 to 1994.

Table 9:   The numbers of employed foreign nationals by trade, 1983-1994

Profession	Number of employed			Change in per cent		
	1983	1990	1994	83-90	90-94	83-94
Experts, technicians	4,082	12,743	18,543	212.2	45.5	354.3
Managers	1,483	3,465	4,597	133.7	32.7	210.0
Officials	1,508	2,592	3,222	71.9	24.3	113.7
Trade and shops	2,743	4,100	6,176	49.5	50.6	125.2
Domestic service	1,363	1,824	5,332	33.8	192.3	291.2
Agriculture	895	910	1,015	1.7	11.5	13.4
Construction and industries	10,916	23,552	38,714	115.8	64.4	254.7
Total	22,990	49,186	77,599	114.0	57.8	237.5

Source: Servico de Estrangeiros e Fronteiras.[9]

This demonstrates that it was particularly when the economy was first opened that the Portuguese labour force needed foreign labour, and that the demand was comparatively greatest for people with a high level of education. As far as professionals, technicians and managers are concerned, there has been a falling off in demand, which could be the result of national education and training schemes being implemented that have reduced the need to import labour in these areas. It could also be that the requirement for importation of labour was especially large at the start of the expansion phase.[10] It is in the area of the highly educated that the percentage fall in the number of foreign nationals is greatest, while the fall in the number of unskilled labourers in industry and construction is more modest. However, there is a clear percentage rise in the number of foreign nationals employed in domestic service.

The highly educated foreign labour was mainly recruited in the other EU States, North America and Brazil, while the demand for unskilled labourers was mostly filled from the former colonies in Africa.[11] The significance of foreign labour in relation to the national labour force can be seen from Table 10. In the group of experts and technicians, foreign nationals comprised 2.98% of the labour force in 1991, and 3.80% in the group of directors and managers, while in the other groups the proportion of foreign nationals is under 1%, apart from industry and construction where 1.65% are foreign nationals.

Table 10:   The labour force in Portugal by trade, 1991

Profession	Labour force	Aliens	Percentage aliens in labour force
Experts and technicians	467,000	13,927	2.98
Directors and managers	101,100	3,839	3.80
White-collar workers	623,400	2,682	0.43
Trade and shops	478,200	4,285	0.90
Domestic service	597,400	2,148	0.36
Agriculture	808,200	902	0.11
Construction and industries	1,488,100	24,517	1.65
Not classified	66,100	2,639	-
Total	4,629,500	54,939	1.19

Source: Servico de Estrangeiros e Fronteiras.[12]

These figures do not reflect illegal labour immigration, which in 1993 was estimated to comprise between 40,000 and 60,000 people.[13] In other words, the number of illegal workers roughly corresponds to the number of foreign workers with labour permits. In order to understand the problems concerning illegal labour immigrants, it is necessary to look more closely at the structure of the Portuguese labour market.

Developments in the Portuguese labour market are moving towards dual segmentation. As far as the importation into Portugal of unskilled labour immigrants is concerned, legal as well as illegal, this mainly occurs in the sector where labour is vulnerable in terms of pay, conditions and career opportunities. It is here we find concentrations of both legal and illegal unskilled labour immigrants. They lack professional qualifications and, not least, the social contacts which play a significant role in gaining access to the sector with good pay, conditions and career opportunities. They have an additional handicap in their lack of knowledge of Portuguese. A factor such as discrimination against foreigners also plays a marginalising role.

In attempts to surmount the barriers to finding jobs, numbers of legal unskilled foreign nationals are forced to work in the "black" sector, where all the illegal labour immigrants are also found. They try to manage via their own internal family social network. They accept the pay and conditions they can get, because they concentrate on saving up, and many have not yet developed a habit for such a high standard of living as unskilled workers amongst the majority of the population.

Various estimates have been made of the number of illegal immigrants, all people without residence permits being included here. Table 11 gives an estimate of the number of illegal immigrants classified by country of origin. There is heavy over-representation of Africans, especially from the former Portuguese colonies. It is thought that they are chiefly employed in unskilled work, as the men mostly work in construction and manufacturing, while the women, of whom there are not so many, are especially associated with cleaning work.[14]

Table 11 is based on information from SEF (Foreigner Service Data) combined with other sources, Census 1991, the Associations of Immigrants and indirectly the Extraordinary Regularization Process of Immigrants (1992/1993).[15]

Table 11: Provisional estimate of the number of illegal immigrants in Portugal, by country of origin

Angola	10,000	-15,000	25%
Cap Verde	8,000	-12,000	20%
Guinea Bissau	8,000	-12,000	20%
St. Principe	1,600	-2,400	4%
Brazil	4,000	-6,000	11%
Others	8,000	-12,000	20%
Total	40,000	-60,000	100%

Source: Maria Beatriz Rocha-Trindade, Portugal: The New Framework of Migration Policies (1993).

Investigations into conditions in the construction industry show that underpayment, lack of holiday savings and of insurance against accident or illness, and frequent dismissals, are common in this sector.[16] Table 12 illustrates employment developments in the construction industry in the period 1990-1994. An increasing number of workers in legal employment are employed on short-term contracts. In 1990, 67% were employed on short-term contracts; this proportion had increased to 72.3% in 1994. The number of permanently employed construction workers fall from 33.9% in 1991 to 27.7% in 1994. The number of people working in the informal economy was estimated at 29.6% in 1991 and 19.4% in 1994. This fall may be due to numbers having acquired a green card. The number of workers with green cards, who are officially self-employed, rose from 18.4% in 1990 to 27.4% in 1994.[17] They must pay tax and social contributions themselves, but in reality they form a part of the labour force in the same way as other skilled and unskilled workers in the construction industry.

In certain urban centres (amongst others Lisbon) the Building Workers Federation estimates that up to half the labour force are foreign nationals. This is an area where workplaces shift from site to site and where working conditions are bad. The decline in the number of people employed in the informal economy in the period from 1990 to 1994 is considered to be partially due to the trade union campaign against "black" labour and partially that many workers obtained a green card.[18]

The demand for labour in the construction industry was partly due to the building of housing, but more to the building of banks, hotels, shopping malls, motorways and other roads. In order to reduce costs and risks, large companies in the construction industry increasingly developed a system of subcontractors who are responsible for finding workers and putting them to work.[19] Some of these subcontractors have Africans as suppliers who can recruit labour quickly through their personal networks. The responsibility for pay and conditions is uncertain and obscure in this system, where each subcontractor strives to make a profit. Pay levels have been seen for "black" labour under 60% of that agreed by the main contractor. Middlemen appropriate the remaining 40%. "Black" labour also exists in construction carried out for the State. Both private and State employers benefit by using "black" labour. It keeps pay costs down in general and makes it cheaper for both private people and the State to build.[20]

Table 12:   Building trades manning 1990-1994

	1990		1991		1992		1993	
	Number	%	Number	%	Number	%	Number	%
Legal employees	183,383	52.0	186,376	54.2	192,954	58.9	179,973	53.2
Short-term contracts	122,956	67.0	127,194	68.2	137,815	71.4	130,173	72.3
Long-term contracts	60,427	33.0	59,182	31.8	55,022	28.6	49,800	27.7
"Black"	104,367	29.6	81,824	23.8	57,146	17.4	62,527	19.4
Workers total	287,750	81.6	268,200	78.0	250,100	76.3	245,500	72.6
Green card workers	65,080	18.4	75,615	22.0	77,663	23.7	92,600	27.4
Total	352,830	100.0	343,815	100.0	327,763	100.0	338,100	100.0
Illegal/legal	0.57		0.44		0.30		0.35	

Source: Annual Report of the Bank of Portugal; Employees tables of the Ministry of Employment; National Federation of the Trade Unions of construction, Wood and Marble Stone.[21]

The Portuguese trade union movement is weak. Membership is low and the system with several levels of subcontractors makes it difficult to recruit members to the unions. The unions are reluctant to report cases of "black" labour to the inspectors, because sanctions mainly hit illegal migrant workers.

Though the use of "black" labour is especially well organised in the construction industry, illegal migrant workers are also found in restaurants, shops, trading in the streets, and especially as cleaners in industry and private homes.[22]

Despite the requirements of the Schengen agreement for increased border controls and the combating of illegal immigration, the demand for labour in certain sections of the Portuguese economy contributes to the continuation of importation of illegal migrant workers. Discussions are currently going on about regulating their status and making them legal. In the weak Portuguese trade unions, demands have been made for sanctions to be applied for breaking the regulations, which should affect everyone in the chain of contractors and subcontractors who are obviously exploiting immigrants. A ban on the use of "black" labour in connection with major construction work has also been demanded.

Developments in Germany

As an example of an EU country with high pay levels and a social security system paid for by the employers, we will look at conditions in Germany.

As in the majority of the former industrial countries, West Germany has experienced a change in the pattern of employment over the last 50 years. Originally, the primary sector dominated. This domination was succeeded by the secondary sector, and in recent years the tertiary sector has been dominant.[23] According to Blossfeld, Gianelli and Mayer, the change in Germany has been somewhat different from that in the majority of other countries, in that German wage-earners less often move from one sector to another. Changes in the employment structure have largely been caused by young people entering the service sector, while migration from the former dominant sector has taken place through old people retiring.[24]

Several factors are thought to explain this. The German educational system of "Volkschule", "Realschule" and "Gymnasium", in combination with professional training, determines people's position in the employment structure, with little room for flexibility. Another factor is that the employment structure in companies is less differentiated than in many other countries, the number of opportunities for mobility therefore being fewer. A third factor, which contributes to keeping people in secure employment positions, is the works councils. Every company with ten or more employees has a works council that wields a significant influence on appointments and dismissals, which means that involuntary dismissals are very limited. It can be expensive for a company to change the make-up of its personnel.[25]

Finally, the German social insurance system has helped to cement noticeable differences in the employment structure. Germany was one of the first countries to combat the trade union movement by adopting a paternalistic welfare insurance system.[26] Under this system, manual and white-collar workers each had their own insurance schemes, creating a wide social division between the two groups that is not usually crossed by new appointments and transfers. The restructuring in the pattern of employment has to a large extent, therefore, only been possible because the State made it possible in the 1960s and 1970s for a growing number of wage-earners to retire rather than finding another position in the employment structure.[27] Despite these barriers, developments in Germany follow the general pattern for former industrial countries in that employment in the tertiary sector has become increasingly dominant.

Until 1973, West Germany was Western Europe's largest importer of foreign labour, and in this connection stress should be placed on the word "foreign". In official reports, the massive importation of people from former East Germany since the end of World War II is not included, nor are people of German origin from the former Soviet Union. All people of German extraction are automatically reckoned to be citizens of the former West Germany. In official statistics, "foreign labour" is therefore restricted to everyone not of German extraction.

The importation of foreign labour started with the import of workers from Italy in 1955. This was quickly extended to include countries such as Spain, Portugal, Tunisia, Yugoslavia, Morocco and Turkey. The importation continued until 1973, when laws were passed to stop new labour permits being issued. Despite this, numbers of foreigners rose sharply as a result of the reunion of families, natural growth and an influx of political refugees. It has since continued in various ways.

Germany has never officially recognised that it is a country of immigration, and it was only in 1991 that politicians stated that foreigners should be integrated and be allowed to take German citizenship. It has been and still is difficult for people of non-German origin to achieve citizenship. The stated policy contains three principles:

1) Integration of foreigners living legally in Germany. This applies especially to immigrant labourers and their relatives;
2) Restrictions on further immigration from countries outside the EU; and
3) Support for repatriation and reintegration in their native countries.

According to Cyrus, the main message is that Germany will not be a country of immigration.[28] Attempts have been made for years to limit the influx of refugees by tightening asylum laws, as for instance in 1993.

In June 1993, 2,184,000 foreigners were employed in Germany. Of these, 26.5% came from other EU countries and 73.5% from countries outside the EU. The largest groups of foreign nationals are 28.9% (632,000) Turks, 19.1% (418,000) from former Yugoslavia, 8.9% (194,000) from Italy and 5.5% (120,000) from Greece. In all, it is estimated that 8.9% (around 7 million) of the population in Germany are foreigners.

The figures for immigration and emigration are interesting. In 1989, 771,000 foreigners came into the country while 438,000 left it. This gave a positive balance of immigration of 323,000. Compared with the natural growth of the German population, where the death rate exceeds the birth rate by approximately 300,000, immigration thus balances losses resulting from the negative natural growth.

The percentage of foreigners with legal residence permit constituted 9.6% of the labour force. Of these, 11.7% were employed in manufacturing, 13.7% in construction, 14.4% in mining, 15% in iron and steel production and 23.4% in foundries, 13.2% in the car industry, 29.6% in hotels and catering, and 23.6% in cleaning work. These industries could scarcely manage without foreign labour.

Unemployment in the population as a whole was 9.2%, while among foreigners it was 16.2%. They suffer from the same marginalisation as in other EU countries, due to their lack of knowledge of German, technical qualifications, social qualifications, etc., and to discrimination. The number of foreign women on low incomes is much higher than that of foreign men and German women, due to foreign women mainly being employed in low-paid service work. Among German women, 4.9% work in cleaning jobs, while the corresponding figure for foreign women is 14.4%.

Despite the ban on issuing new labour permits in 1973, the flow of labour from non-EU countries has never fully stopped. Specialists, etc., have been able to immigrate and there are currently many exceptions, but foreigners who are allowed in receive time-restricted permits making it impossible for them to take up permanent residence in Germany, as used to be the case.

Non-EU citizens can be issued with a labour permit for a specific job for up to one year if the authorities consider that there are not enough qualified people in Germany to carry out the work in question. These are often jobs with poor pay and conditions, commonly part-time jobs in the cleaning sector. These latter normally belong to a category known as "unprotected jobs" since, due to short hours and low pay, no social security contributions need to be paid.

Since 1991 the authorities have allowed a quota of Eastern European citizens time-limited jobs on contract. Each year the German government specifies how many contract workers a specific number of Eastern European countries may send to Germany. By law, these contract workers must receive the same pay as German workers but pay tax and social insurance in their homelands. Several investigations show that they actually receive lower pay. The amount they have to pay in tax and social security to their homeland is often less than in Germany so in many cases workers receive a lower wage: a clear example of "social dumping". The system of contract workers is therefore resisted by the trade unions because it is thought to contribute to low wages in the construction industry, where large numbers of contract workers are employed.

In 1993 the number of non-EU citizens from Eastern Europe with temporary labour permits comprised 181,037 permits for seasonal work, 68,522 for contract work, 7,771 for guest workers and 5,990 for cross-border workers. The corresponding figures for 1994 were 155,217 for seasonal work, 36,108 for contract work and 5,529 for guest workers.[29] There is thus a fairly significant importation of labour from the Eastern European countries during a period when many people who would be able to perform this work are unemployed in other EU countries.

According to Cyrus, it is an increasingly widely held apprehension amongst employers and authorities that German pay costs are too high compared with other countries and that a reduction in pay is necessary in order to maintain Germany's ability to compete. This opinion had difficulty gaining recognition in the normal labour market, but in recent years a development has taken place of various atypical employment conditions in which contributions to social security have been increasingly shifted to the individual employee. This has resulted in low pay costs for employers. Amongst other things Cyrus names the contract worker arrangement with the various Eastern European countries, leasing arrangements for labour, the re-categorisation of workers as independently self-employed, the recruitment of labour via subcontractors, and short-term employment for seasonal work.

Under the new rules, Germany ensures its ability to import labour when needed. It also ensures that this labour can be sent back when it is no longer needed. Finally, the legislation protects German workers, as foreigners must have the same pay and conditions. A large bureaucracy is necessary to administer the new rules for temporary immigration.

Despite tightened border controls, the German police estimate that about 100,000 people a year enter Germany illegally. In 1993, the police caught some 24,000 people trying to cross the border illegally. The majority were Romanians. Many enter the country legally on visas and short-term contracts and remain there. The German Ministry of the Interior estimates that in 1990 there were around 100,000 people residing illegally in West Germany while voluntary aid organisations estimate that there were 100,000 in Berlin alone.

These figures seem very low. Cyrus states that around 500,000 Polish "tourists" are officially estimated to be working illegally in Germany. Not a lot is known about the informal economy in Germany. It has been estimated that the number of people working "black" is between 100,000 and 600,000. The German trade unions estimate that the number of people performing "black" labour is about 500,000. How many of these are foreigners is not known, and how many are illegal immigrants is even more uncertain. However, we know that since 1988 the number of cases discovered of illegal employment of foreigners has grown. In 1991, 36,661 cases of illegal employment of foreigners were registered, resulting in fines of DM 333,144. In 1992, the number of cases had risen to 44,800. Illegal employment of foreigners mainly takes place in small and medium-sized companies. They are mostly employed in the construction industry and in the hotel and restaurant trade. They accept work for low wages and do not pay social security.

The use of illegal immigrants as "black" labourers is, however, not limited to small and medium-sized companies. Various sources[30] have revealed that large concerns often delegate work to subcontractors in order to reduce production costs. These subcontractors are often based outside the EU and supply the main contractor with labour from third countries at very low prices. In some cases it is even profitable to use EU citizens in this way. Thus we have examples of Portuguese brewery workers being brought to Germany and Belgium to work for extremely low wages, without social security contributions being made for them since they are insured at home. This is another instance of social dumping.

"Migration News" reports many examples of Dutch construction companies establishing branches in Portugal and then collaborating with German companies to supply labour. In accordance with the deal with the German firms, the Portuguese workers should receive DM 20-30 an hour. However, the workers only received DM 6-8, the Dutch company keeping the rest.[31]

In England and Portugal it is comparatively easy to be registered as self-employed, and it is a well-known fact that many English construction workers travelled to Germany where they work officially as self-employed, but in reality work as though they were employed in a firm (i.e. under supervision). By being self-employed, they can set their own pay levels, and are personally responsible for paying taxes and social security contributions. They are therefore able to work for less than the normal wages. The German trade unions maintain that they are not really self-employed and exempt from paying tax deducted at source and observing minimum wage levels, but in reality illegally supervised at the German workplace and not members of the German Construction Employers Federation.

In order to combat the illegal employment of foreigners, from January 1st, 1990 all employers have been required to check whether their employees have a valid social security card. Foreigners working in the construction industry, cleaning, setting up and taking down exhibitions, etc., are required to carry their social security card on them and produce on demand. Aliens living illegally in Germany cannot obtain such a card. Employers caught employing foreigners illegally must pay for their deportation, plus a fine.

The German Labour Inspectorate is responsible for combating the employment of illegal labour immigrants, and in collaboration with large police forces checks are frequently made of building sites, hotels and restaurants. According to "Migration News", Germany spends more on preventing illegal immigration than any other country. The country has 1,500 inspectors and the Ministry of Labour spends DM 150 million a year in combating illegal immigration and abuse of social security. This does not include the expense of police support. Attempts are being made to intensify these efforts. Until now, Berlin has had 43 inspectors but during the next two years this force will be expanded by 150. A raid on 3,600 firms in the restaurant trade during March 1995 found that 23% employed illegal labour immigrants, 43% of the approximately 15,000 employees were foreigners, of whom 22% were illegal immigrants.[32]

To sum up, it can be seen that developments are under way in the German labour market in the form of atypical employment conditions for foreign labour, where attempts are being made to reduce wages. This affects both foreigners residing and working legally in Germany as well as illegal immigrants. Research into these conditions is in many ways inadequate, but there is no doubt that the authorities are spending significant sums in combating illegal employment and underpayment in the construction industry, agriculture and the restaurant trade, whereas little has been written about illegal labour in the domestic sector.

Developments in Denmark

As an example of an EU country with a high level of wages, a Nordic labour market model and a State financed social welfare system, we shall now look at conditions in Denmark.

Denmark began to import foreign labour later after World War II than most other countries in Central and Northern Europe. Throughout most of the 1960s, departure from agriculture, resulting from rationalisation and extensive mobilisation of housewives, satisfied the labour requirements of industry and the growing service sector. Not until 1967 did it become difficult to obtain workers for the labour market, and the unions agreed to permit importation of labour from abroad, provided the workers received the same conditions as Danes and that labour permits would only be issued if qualified Danish workers could not be found.[33]

This happened at the same time as West Germany suffered a temporary recession, resulting in some aliens losing their jobs. Instead of returning home, some of them looked for jobs in neighbouring countries. This is how the first Turks and Moroccans came to Denmark. A year later, Pakistani workers also came looking for work. In a few companies in the Danish metal-working industry which were desperately short of labour, employers themselves travelled to Yugoslavia to recruit labour. Those who arrived in Denmark first were encouraged by their employers to write home to relatives and friends who were looking for work, and a number of chain migrations from Turkey, Pakistan, Morocco and Yugoslavia quickly developed.

In the 1970s, the influx of foreigners looking for work expanded greatly. Fearing that demand would exceed the supply of available jobs, the Danish authorities decided to introduce a temporary stop on issue of new first-time labour permits on November 5th, 1970.[34] Legislation was introduced giving immigrants already living here the opportunity to bring in wives, children and parents, and in some cases employers could be granted dispensation to import labour. On January 1st, 1973, Denmark joined the Common Market, excluding citizens of the other Common Market countries from the ban on immigration. In 1973 the temporary ban on immigration was lifted for a short period, but a total ban was introduced that November.[35] Immigrants already living here could still bring in their families, and dispensations could be granted in certain circumstances. The rules governing family reunions have been tightened several times since, most recently in 1992.[36]

In January 1971, 49,811 people were living in Denmark who were citizens of countries outside Scandinavia. By January 1st, 1996, this had risen to 195,772 while at the same time numbers of foreign citizens had been naturalised. No precise figures are available as to how many naturalisations have taken place since January 1st, 1971, but from January 1st, 1979 to January 1st, 1994, 58,552 people were naturalised. Between 1974 and 1978, 12,350 people were granted Danish citizenship. The growth in the number of foreigners since the ban was introduced in November 1970 is partly due to family reunions and partly to refugees being granted asylum. A few have been granted labour permits in accordance with the strict rules for dispensation and there has also been a natural growth.

On January 1st, 1994, 3.6% of the population were aliens. Of these, 19% came from the other Nordic countries, EU countries and North America, while the remaining 71% came from so-called "third" countries. The largest group was from Turkey. On January 1st, 1994, there were 34,658 Turkish citizens in Denmark.

Figure 11: The Danish workforce by sector

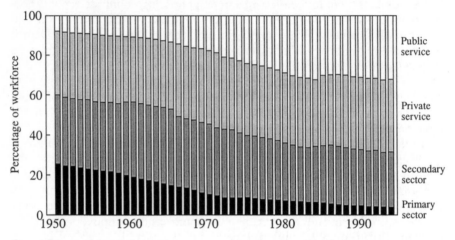

Source: Danmarks Statistik.

Originally large numbers of labour migrants found work in Greater Copenhagen, but they soon began to appear in metal-casting firms and other metal industries in the provinces. In many cases this was in companies unable to attract Danish workers because of pay and employment conditions.

When the crisis began in the middle of the 1970s, a number of these companies closed and in many cases the migrant workers moved to neighbouring towns, hoping for better chances of finding work. As a result, concentrations arose in Aarhus, Odense and the Greater Copenhagen area. At the same time as numbers of labour immigrants increased as a result of family reunions and natural growth, the number of political refugees also rose. As these were granted asylum, politicians have tried to introduce a policy of spreading them about the country in order to achieve a more equal division of the burdens connected with integration and to prevent the development of concentrations of refugees in socially depressed areas in the cities.[37] This policy of dispersing refugees has mostly been successful, nevertheless over half of all foreign nationals in Denmark live round Copenhagen, and in Copenhagen itself they constituted 9% of the population on January 1st, 1994.

In 1993, foreign citizens constituted 2.5% of the total workforce but nearly 7% of the total number of unemployed. Unemployment is significantly higher among foreign nationals than in the population as a whole, and for certain nationalities it is 3-4 times higher. 50-75% have unstable employment and are hit by unemployment more often than the workforce as a whole. When foreign citizens become unemployed, they have great difficulty finding new work. They belong to the B team with a vengeance.

The majority of foreign nationals from "third" countries are employed as unskilled workers and only a few in white-collar jobs. The majority of foreigners from "third" countries are employed on unskilled work in manu-facturing companies. They often have the kind of jobs that Danish workers do not want because wages are low and the working hours are inconvenient or because the working conditions are dirty and unsanitary. They are commonly employed in small firms whose owner is not a member of the Danish Federation of Employers. They normally receive pay corresponding to the rates in the collective agreements. Much of the work the foreign workers originally performed has disappeared, either because the com-panies closed as a result of the crisis, or because rationalisation took place that made them superfluous. Foreign women are not employed in manu-facturing industry as much as men, the majority working in the service sector. Social mobility has been extremely limited, though in recent years a low grade of mobility has occurred as a result of the need for bilingual employees in schools, kindergartens and other social institutions.

Since their arrival at the end of the 1960s, immigrants have been em-ployed in low-paid, dirty and uncomfortable work in jobs sensitive to eco-nomic fluctuation. Those in employment are still chiefly linked to this sec-tor. When they become unemployed, they have great difficult in finding new jobs. This can be due to language factors and inadequate technical qualifications. Language problems do not apply to the many young people who have grown up in this country. They speak Danish and went to school in Denmark, but they still find it very difficult to get jobs. Like the older labour immigrants, they are handicapped by their lack of social connections to employees in successful companies, and they are discriminated against because of their ethnic background.

To a great extent, discrimination is a result of the negative attitude to foreigners that developed since the crisis set in at the beginning of the 1970s. When Denmark opened up for the importation of labour at the end of the 1960s, many people regarded them as positive. Foreigners came to help maintain economic growth. Without them, many firms would have had to close or move abroad. Many people looked on foreign workers in this positive light, but were well aware that they would find it difficult to settle in culturally and socially. However, these were considered minor problems compared with the advantages gained in having them. Most Danes expected them to go home when there was no longer work for them, and the immigrants also expected this. To prevent them from getting into social difficulties if they became unemployed, a law was passed which required them to join an unemployment fund for a minimum of two years when their first labour permit was granted. To a great extent this demand was obeyed, and since unemployment funds are administered by the local trade unions, many also joined a union.

When the recession started in the 1970s, it triggered violent pressure on social payments to unemployment benefits, social security benefits and others. Taxes rose and competition ensued between State and private consumption. Many Danes wanted lower taxes, but at the same time wished to keep the social benefits. This resulted in a contradictory situation, since it is not logically possible to fulfil both desires at the same time.

Some politicians exploited this situation to whip up a negative attitude towards immigrants and refugees by maintaining that immigrants and refugees were an economic drain on Danish society because so many of them were unemployed.[38] The picture of immigrants and refugees as an economic drain on and a threat to the social welfare system spread and has given rise to negative attitudes in certain circles. Combined with the fact that many Danes no longer meet foreigners at work nor have other social contacts with them, many people are totally ignorant about them, allowing the spread of myths.

Like other former industrial countries, Denmark has contributed to an international export of capital to areas with low wage levels. Numbers of Danish companies engaged in the manufacture of shoes and textiles have transferred part of their production of finished and semi-finished goods to Portugal in order to benefit from low Portuguese wage levels. As far as I know, there has not been any investigation as to what this parcelling out to foreign countries has meant to the number of jobs in Denmark. A leading member of staff in one of Denmark's larger companies told me, however, that his company had become more competitive in both quality and price by sending some phases of production to Portugal. This resulted in the company achieving a greater share of the international market. Production has risen and this, combined with the contracted out work, led to a significant expansion in the number of highly trained employees at the head office in Denmark. The new employees are highly paid designers, planners and marketing experts. The director estimated that laying out had resulted in a doubling of the number of administrative staff at home, besides creating jobs in Portugal for Danes in management.

In the labour market in Denmark, it can be seen that since the early 1970s there has been a noticeable reduction in the number of jobs in manufacturing industry in the Greater Copenhagen area, at the same time as there has been growth in the number of employees in both private and public service sectors. Developments in numbers of new jobs in manufacturing have mainly taken place in the provinces.[39] In 1987, 67% of jobs in the country were in service trades. In the Copenhagen region, three-quarters of those employed in work in service industries such as banks, insurance companies and business services. Especially the group of business service companies, which includes advertising, consultancy, computing, architectural work, legal work, marketing, etc., experienced an almost explosive growth until 1987.[40] In 1988, just over half the jobs in the area round the capital were in this sector. In the largest provincial towns, especially Aarhus, jobs in business services also dominated. Two-thirds of Denmark's jobs in business services are based in the area round the capital and in Aarhus, Odense and Aalborg!

Figure 12: **Self-employed workers as a percentage of the labour force in Denmark. Men and women broken down by nationality, 1980-1994**

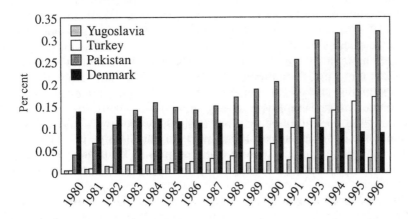

Source: Danmarks Statistik.

The number of jobs in industry in the area round the capital went down by more than a third over the last 20 years. The decline was especially great in Copenhagen itself. Forecasts for the metropolitan region show that in the industrial sector a small growth is expected in the paper and graphic industry and the chemical industry, while manufacturing companies as a whole are expected to experience a recession. Significant growth is expected in the hotel and catering trade, with less growth in the transport sector, which includes all land, sea and air transport. Banking and finance, post and telecommunications, and insurance companies are expected to maintain a relatively stable level of employment, while business services will experience a noticeable advance, as will recreation and sport.[41]

All the central organisations for economy, politics, communication and research are concentrated in the area round the capital. In 1989, nearly 70% of funds for research were spent in the Copenhagen area, and this applies as much to the State research effort (70.1%) as to private efforts (67.7%). Large numbers of jobs in high technological industry are found in the area round the capital. In 1988, 58% of the total number of high technological jobs in Denmark was involved here. There is also a concentration of museums, theatres, festivals, congresses, exhibitions and shows, sights, hotels and restaurants, and a strong international orientation.[42] A number of international hotel chains have established themselves and the area is also well covered by congress centres.

Ethnically, most concerns are started by Danes, but in major towns, where most of the immigrants live, many refugees and immigrants have started their own businesses. In 1980, 13.86% of Danish citizens who were active in the labour market were self-employed. By 1994, this figure had fallen to 10.06%. In comparison, it should be mentioned that in 1990, 6.77% of Turkish nationals, 2.59% of nationals of Yugoslavia and 20.58% of Pakistani nationals were self-employed. By 1994 these figures had risen to 14.13% for Turkish nationals, 3.53% for nationals from former Yugoslavia and 31.49% for Pakistani nationals.[43] There is uneven growth in the number of self-employed among immigrant groups from Pakistan and Turkey, and these figures may not even show the true picture. There are grounds for assuming that if the many Pakistani immigrants who have taken Danish citizenship are included, the proportion of independent self-employed among people of Pakistani origin would be over 31.49% (see Figure 12).

If this development continues, it will mean that the number of firms owned by members of the new ethnic minorities will grow. No studies exist of the economic and social implications of these companies. The number of self-employed is particularly high amongst immigrants from Turkey and Pakistan, where the majority have their origins in rural country societies where they grew up in families that were self-employed. In a group such as immigrants from former Yugoslavia, the majority were recruited by Danish employers travelling to Skopje and Pristina to find welders, smiths, mechanics and unskilled industrial labourers. Many of these immigrants had a background as wage-earners before migrating to Denmark, and they have not established themselves as self-employed to the same extent as immigrants from Pakistan and Turkey who came to Denmark at the same time. It may therefore be possible to explain this difference by referring to the different lifestyles in the three groups, but more empirical research is necessary before this assumption can be confirmed.

Throughout the past 20 years, Denmark has had a relatively high level of unemployment that the current economic and political structures have been unable to solve, but looking at the number of people in employment in the active age group between 18 to 66 during the period from 1960 to 1995, the figure has remained fairly constant at about 70-75%.[44] The burden of providing for the non-working part of the Danish population has not changed. In 1960 the family took care of the non-working part of the population. A change has since taken place, an increasing share of these provisions having passed to the authorities.[45] In 1970, about 7% of the total population were dependent on State income support. This figure had risen to 24% in 1992 and forecasts of population growth show that if the welfare system is not changed, the support burden will grow even more in the future.[46] The support burden has not changed, but much of the work that used to be performed in the home, such as looking after children and old people, is now carried out by the labour market and in many cases requires a family to have two incomes.

In the late 1960s and early 1970s, while there was full employment, Denmark developed a relatively generous welfare system, especially as far as unemployment benefits, social security payments and pensions were concerned. At best, unemployed people can receive benefits corresponding to 90% of their former pay, though with a maximum of 90% of the average pay in the labour market covered by private collective agreements. As mentioned previously, this caused neo-liberal researchers such as Peder Pedersen and Nina Smith to believe that workers at the lower end of the pay scale can rightly ask themselves whether it can pay to work.[47]

The question of whether there is no disincentive to work if, as unemployed, a massive State provision can be received which is only 10% less than the income received from working, is hypothetical since there are not jobs for everyone. The only time in Denmark's history when there were jobs for everyone was at the end of the 1960s and at that time just about everyone who was fit was in employment. As mentioned, a questionnaire investigation carried out by the Rockwool Foundation in 1993-94 showed that among the employed, about 3% of men and 8% of women "lost" disposable income by going to work while around 17% earned less than DKK 500 by going to work instead of receiving full unemployment benefit.[48] There are therefore some 28% who receive no significant economic benefit from working. Despite the lack of an economic incitement, many people do go to work, proving that numbers of non-economic factors play a role.

Politically attempts have been made to prevent "black" labour in the form of cleaning in private houses by introducing a home service arrangement allowing private people who start a home service company to receive a State subsidy of DKK 65 an hour for work performed for private persons. In this way, old people and others who need cleaners, gardeners and so on, get cheap labour which costs roughly the same as "black" labour, and unemployed people get jobs.

In an attempt to reduce wage costs, a tendency has been seen in some branches to replace employees on adult wages by 16-18-year-olds who are paid less. Ingemann and Lind have shown that in shops there has been an increase in the employment of people under 18, for whom minimum wage requirements are extremely low compared with those of people over 18. They found that 59% of companies listed in the Shop and Office Workers Union trade directory employ people under 18. In four subsidiary branches (supermarkets, low price warehouses, discount boutiques and bakers) more than 80% of the companies employ people under the age of 18. Outside bakeries, the employment of people under 18 is most widespread in the convenience goods trade. In kiosks and petrol stations, people under 18 are employed in half. People under 15 constitute only a very small part of those young under 18 in the area studied. In kiosks and discount firms, young people under 18 constitute 25% of the basic labour force. Of these young people, 80% work for between 5 and 15 hours a week. By comparing conditions in 1993 with those in 1995, Ingemann and Lind conclude that "there was no decline in the employment of people under 18 in the course of the 2½ years that passed between the two studies".[49] In the retail trade, the number of young people rose from around 48,000 in 1993 to around 57,000 in 1995, or nearly 20%. Measured as an average number of young people per company, there has been a rise in all sectors except kiosks and petrol stations, which are unchanged. The number of non-trainees among young people working more than 20 hours a week is relatively high in kiosks and petrol stations.[50]

Ingemann and Lind's investigation only includes the employment of young people in commerce and shops, and there is a great need for broader study to include the whole private labour market, even though there is little doubt that young people are mostly employed in commerce and shops. The reason is no doubt linked to the taylorisation of work functions which has taken place in commerce and which has increasingly resulted in the possibility of employing people under 18, thus reducing a company's total wage bill.

The growing employment of young people in commerce and shops may also be linked to the fact that this is a branch with unusually poor cover as far as collective agreements are concerned. In an interesting study, Scheuer has shown that in smaller companies in the private sector with only 1 to 10 employees, only 35% are covered by collective agreements, while for large concerns with over 1,000 employees the corresponding figure is 81%. In 1994, 52% of wage-earners in the private sector were covered by collective agreements, though this figure varied from 65% in the food industry to only 31% in commerce and shops. Scheuer also investigated how many wage earners in the private sector were covered by collective agreements in relation to trade unions. Here Finansforbundet (the Finance Federation) tops with 95% and Kvindeligt Arbejderforbund (the Women Workers' Federation) with 83% while HK (the Shop and Office Workers' Union) only reached 49%. Scheuer's material is unfortunately too restricted to base any conclusions about conditions on it, for instance, the Hotel and Restaurant Workers' Union. It is a branch where it is normally expected that few members are organised. This applies to both employees and employers.[51]

No studies have been carried out of the extent of underpayment in companies without collective agreements. Occasionally the newspapers report instances of this. On March 9th, 1996, Berlingske Tidende carried the following headline: "Shop trainees cheated of pay and days off". From the text it appears that the deputy director of the Dansk Handel og Service (the Danish Trade and Service Association) believed "that the problem is due to non-organised employers who are not familiar with the collective agreements." The article also reveals that "according to the Shop and Office Workers Union, there are problems with the conditions for shop trainees in one shop in three". Furthermore, "it is especially in the smaller boutiques that there are problems, whereas HK rarely encounters cases in the large chain stores".

No studies have been published as to pay conditions for adult wage-earners employed in companies not covered by collective agreements. No laws or regulations exist to stop a person taking a job for a wage under the minimum level for a collective agreement sector, if a company has not entered into a collective agreement. However, the collective agreement's minimum wage level must be assumed to form the norm for the majority of the Danish labour market.

When the recession began to bite at the beginning of the 1970s, and numbers of unemployed rose, people in political circles regarded unemployment as a temporary phenomenon. Those who were hit by unemployment needed to be ensured support at a level which would allow them to maintain a reasonable standard of living until they could find a new job. For the unemployed, this amounted to a sum corresponding to about 90% of the average wage for an unskilled worker. In order to qualify for unemployment benefit or social security payments, the unemployed are obliged to accept work if it is offered.

Gradually, as it became clear that unemployment was not a temporary phenomenon, a number of political measures were taken. At the end of the 1970s, people who had been unemployed for long periods were offered employment for 7 to 9 months after two years' unemployment so that they could maintain their qualifications. These jobs were created by subsidising employment at public and private places of work.

In 1979, early retirement was offered, which became extremely popular among the lower paid and which resulted in a reduction in the number of unemployed older people.

In the 1980s it became possible for long-term unemployed to take educational and training courses, and in 1994 the opportunity was given for people to take leave to look after their children and be paid 80% of the unemployment benefit rate. This was reduced to 70%, in November 1994 and to 60% in 1997. Parental leave is available to parents with children under 9 years of age for a period of 13-52 weeks. For parents with children under one year, the first 26 weeks are a legal right (13 weeks for children over one year). Employers may not dismiss workers on the grounds of such leave. Longer periods up to 52 weeks must be accepted by the employer, who is not obliged to re-employ the person after their leave.

It also became possible for people over the age of 25, who were members of an unemployment scheme and who had been in employment for at least three years, to take training leave with support corresponding to 100% of unemployment benefit. The training leave must last at least one week and at most one year, though unemployed people can take training leave for up to 2 years. The employer must agree to the leave but is not obliged to re-employ the person concerned, nor is he obliged to employ someone else. If he employs an out-of-work person who is undergoing retraining, he could receive a subsidy of DKK 43 an hour in 1994.

Finally, people over the age of 25, who are members of an unemployment scheme and who have been in employment for at least three years can take sabbatical leave for up to one year. The employer must agree to the leave and employ an unemployed person, but is not obliged to

Table 13:   **Persons on social benefits**

Unemployment benefit	273,000
Supplementary benefit	165,000
Early retirement pension	270,000
Rehabilitation	18,000
Bridging pension	112,000
Maternity benefit	36,000
Sickness benefit	38,000
Paid leave	57,000
Student grants	147,000
Total support	1,116,000

re-employ the person. In 1994, a person on leave could receive 80% of the normal unemployment benefit. In November 1994, this was reduced to 70% until 1997, when the rate was reduced to 60%.

A number of these arrangements, such as early retirement and the various leave schemes, do not bear any social stigmatisation, in contrast with being long-term unemployed. In the finance report of 1995, the following information appeared on groups receiving public support.[52]

The number of people on unemployment benefit, 273,000, and on supplementary benefit, 165,000, is unnecessarily large when the social costs connected with the role of unemployed are taken into consideration. It is necessary to re-classify a significant number of these people to roles which, like early retirement and parental and educational leave, are not socially stigmatising. The ultimate goal must be for everyone to be offered a citizen's wage to ensure a fair standard of living.

Notes

1   Foreign investments constituted a positive net growth as a percentage of the GNP of 0.7% in the period 1981-1984, 2.3% in the period 1985-1990, and 3.2% in the period 1991-1992. The corresponding figures for Denmark were all negative: -0.1% in the period 1081-1984, -0.5% in the period 1985-1990 and -0.6% in the period 1991-1992 (Employment Outlook, July 1994, OECD: 160). See also Carlos & Borges 1995.

2   Unemployment was 6.7% on average in the period 1983-1991. In 1992 4.2%, 1993 5.5%, 1994 6.4%. The corresponding figures for Denmark

were 1983-1991 9.2%, 1992 11.2%, 1993 12.2%, 1994 11.0% and 1995 10.5% (Employment Outlook, July 1994, OECD: 6).

3   Rocha-Trindade 1993: 167-169.

4   Carlos & Borges 1995: 5.

5   Carlos & Borges 1995: 8.

6   Carlos & Borges 1995: 5.

7   Carlos & Borges 1995: 25-29.

8   China's take-over of Macau in 1999 is expected to lead to a migration to Portugal. There are about 100,000 people with Portuguese passports who not only have the right to reside in Portugal, but also have the right to take employment in all EU countries. A large number of these 100,000 are of Chinese origin (Carlos & Borges 1995: 9).

9   From Malheiros 1996: 3.

10   It has not been possible to acquire data to shed light on which of these two possibilities is correct.

11   Carlos & Borges 1995: 9-19.

12   From Malheiros 1996: 6.

13   Malheiros 1996: 8.

14   Malheiros 1996.

15   Malheiros 1996: 8.

16   In 1981 it was estimated that about 51% of those in private construction companies and public building works were working "black" (Carlos & Borges 1995: 51).

17   Malheiros 1996.

18   Malheiros 1996.

19   Carlos & Borges 1995: 51.

20   Malheiros 1996.

21   From Malheiros 1996: 10.

22   Malheiros 1996.

23   Erikson & Goldthorpe 1985, Müller 1985, Haller 1989.

24   Blossfeld, Gianelli & Mayer 1993.

25   Carroll & Mayer 1986: 325.

26   Flora 1976, Alber 1982.

27   Mayer & Müller 1986.

28   Cyrus 1994.

29   Cyrus 1994: 120-121. Figures from the Zentralstelle für Arbeitsvermittlung der Bundesanstalt für Arbeit.

30   Köhning & Werquin 1990; Nayer & Nys 1992.

31 "Migration News" Vol. 2. No.8. August 1995: 90.
32 "Migration News" Vol. 2, No. 8. August 1995: 90.
33 Citizens of the other Nordic countries have been free to take up residence and employment in Denmark since 1954.
34 Law no. 203 of 27th May 1970.
35 Law no. 155 of 21st March 1973.
36 Law no. 482 of 24th June 1992. Aliens living in Denmark must have been resident for at least five years and be able to prove they can provide for the applicants.
37 Hjarnø 1991.
38 Schierup 1993.
39 Nielsen, B 1995, Hovedstadsregionens Statistikkontor (1993). Maskell 1994, Illeris 1990, Ministry of the Environment 1992.
40 Ministry of the Environment 1992: 46-48.
41 Hovedstadsregionens Statistikkontor 1993.
42 Ministry of the Environment 1992.
43 Schierup 1993: 108.
44 Lind & Møller 1995: 9-10; Finansredegørelsen 1995: 74.
45 Viby-Mogensen could in one way have gone right back to 1960 and shown that the employment rate for people between the ages of 15 and 64 has been relatively stable at around 70-75%, and that the percentage of the active age group has thus been the same for 35 years. The labour force itself, on the other hand, has risen to 83% in 1994 and unemployment in the period 1960-1994 is mostly due to a growth in participation rate, partly because more women are active and partly because of a fall in activity amongst the young and the old. Much of the work formerly performed in the home by women has now been taken over by the State or the private labour market (Ministry of Finance: Budgetredegørelse 95, Copenhagen 1995).
46 In 1994, nearly 25% of people aged 15-64 received unemployment benefits or some other form of social support as compensation for lack of working income. Less than half were registered as unemployed, so dependency on State support exceeds the registered level of unemployment. The group receiving State benefits mainly because of unemployment includes amongst others the following groups in 1991: people in early retirement (257,000), voluntary early retirement pension arrangements (101,000), people receiving sickness benefits for more than 6 months of the year (31,000) people receiving social

security benefits for more than 6 months of the year (120,000) and people in workfare (90,000) (Lind & Møller 1995: 9).

47 Pedersen & Smith 1995: 31-44. See also: Plough 1994, Plovsing 1994, Petersen & Søndergaard 1994.

48 Among the unemployed, about 6% of men and 10% of women expect their total economy to worsen if they get a job, while 17% of men and 26% of women do not expect it to change their economic situation (Pedersen & Smith 1995: 41-42).

49 Ingemann & Lind 1995: 24-25.

50 Ingemann & Lind 1995.

51 Scheuer 1996.

52 Finansredegørelse 1995: 83.

8 Conclusion

Professor David North's theory that governments in democratic countries will never be able to solve the problem of illegal immigration precisely because they are democratic countries is not correct. In the Nordic countries, a labour market democracy has been developed under which employment of foreigners without labour permits is not only regarded as illegal by law but is also regarded as illegal by the social partners in the labour market, the employers and the employees. Employing foreigners without a labour permit is regarded in Scandinavia as breaking the collective agreements entered into by the trade unions and the employers' federations.

In democratic countries where collective bargaining plays a dominant role in the relationship between employers and employees, it can be expected that any employer breaking the agreement by employing illegal immigrants will be stopped by the trade unions and their own employers' federation. Trade unions can take employers who do not respect the collective agreements to the industrial tribunal, and their own federation will not support them. If an employer cannot be brought to order in this way, more serious methods such as strikes or blockades can be used. If the trade union movement and employers' federation are strong, they can prevent individual employers taking on illegal labour immigrants and breaking collective agreements without cost to the State.

In States where collective bargaining plays a lesser role in the relationship between employers and employees, it can be expected that the State will play a larger role in attempts to prevent employment of illegal immigrants. The State may send out inspectors, possibly with police support, to work-sites to carry out checks. It can be extremely expensive to carry out such control and bring employers breaking the law to court.

The analysis above has also shown that the structure of the "black" labour market plays an important role in phenomena such as illegal labour immigration. The demand for illegal labour immigrants will depend on the type of labour needed in the "black" sector and on the way this labour is recruited. The demand for labour varies from country to country and depends on developments in the society concerned. A modern Nordic welfare economy with a high rate of activity among women and a well-developed system of day care for children and young people will limit the demand for unskilled "black" labour in private households, an important market for illegal labour immigrants in less organised countries.[1] Since the recruitment of labour to the informal economy is largely based on social contacts between employers and employees, illegal labour immigrants will have difficulty finding employment. All EU States have an informal economy, which requires more thorough study than was possible in this current work.

Published analyses have also revealed that Saskia Sassen's theory on Global Cities is not a general one. Sassen's assumption that restructuring in the global economy will lead to the formation of powerful global cities is correct on many points. However, on one point her theory does not hold water, and this is her assertion about the development of an extremely low-paid section in the service sector. Such a development only occurs in countries with an undeveloped democracy in the labour market.

In countries such as the USA, for instance, which do not have such a highly developed democratic system with collective bargaining to regulate relations between employers and employees, market forces dominate. The USA lacks a far-reaching democracy in the labour market to ensure close and fruitful co-operation between capital and labour able to create those equal opportunities in pay, conditions and training which are necessary in the long run to ensure trade and industry the flexibility and competitiveness essential for a society to be able to manage competition in line with the extensive restructuring taking place in the global economy. In the USA, restructuring of the global economy with its consequent de-industrialisation has weakened the trade union movement so that it no longer has the necessary political power to combat the steady erosion of the State welfare system. The weakest section of the labour force has been forced out into such great social need and poverty that it has been forced to take employment for pay and conditions which make it impossible ever to break out of poverty. The social consequences are well-known: rising cultural callousness, increasing violence, growing drug addiction, escalating crime, triggering calls for tighter law and order, less freedom and limitations in the democracy for which the USA, on a global level, has made itself the standard-bearer.

Sassen's global city hypothesis has, in many areas, given us a precise understanding of the consequences which the restructuring of the global economy contains for developments in some of the great former industrial metropolises. However, in her model she overlooked the fact that in some areas there are dual developments. The development does not, therefore, necessarily lead to the creation of an extremely low-paid section in the service sector. In countries where conditions in the labour market are controlled by highly developed democratic collaboration between capital and labour, scope is created for a greater degree of economic equality between citizens, with a positive effect on productivity which ensures against social need and poverty, and the evil consequences these engender in the form of violence, criminality, addiction and a strengthened law and order policy which threatens democracy.

There is a need for more empirical and theoretical research into Sassen's global city hypothesis, but on the background of the above brief analysis, much suggests that in the future it could be profitable for political decision-makers to differentiate between "the American way" and "the Danish way" towards a global city.

Note

1 In a country like Denmark, the possibility to exist as an illegal immigrant is limited because of the CPR system (a registration system, where everybody has a personal identity number). Medical aid, police, banks, insurance companies, etc., require evidence of a CPR number.

Bibliography

Alber, Jens (1982)
  Vom Armenhaus zum Wohlfahrtsstaat: Analysen zur Entwicklung der Sozialversicherung in Westeuropa. Frankfurt a.m.: Campus.
Albæk, Karsten, Erik Strøjer Madsen & Kurt Pedersen (1992)
  Veje til fuld beskæftigelse, in Albæk, K et al: *Kampen mod ledigheden,* Spektrum.
Alesina, Alberto & Dani Rodrik (1994)
  Ulighed bidrager til indførelse af væksthæmmende politik. *Quarterly Journal of Economics.* 109 (2).
Andersen, Bent Rold (1991)
  Velfærdsstaten i Danmark og Europa. København: Fremad.
Banton, Michael (1994)
  Discrimination. Buckingham: Open University Press.
Bell, Daniel (1976)
  The Coming of Post-Industrial Society. 2nd ed. New York: Basic Books.
Bensman, Joseph & Arthur J. Vidich (ed) (1960)
  Small town in mass society: class, power, and religion in a rural community. New York: Anchor Books.
Birdsall, Nancy, David Ross & Richard Sabot (1995)
  Investeringer i uddannelse er en nøgle til vedligeholdende vækst, fordi det både bidrager direkte gennem produktivitetseffekten, og fordi det reducerer indkomstulighed. *The World Bank Review.* Vol. 9, no. 3.
Blau, Peter Michael (1964)
  Exchange and power in social life. New York: John Wiley.
Blossfeld, Hans-Peter, Gianna Gianelli & Karl Ulrich Mayer (1993)
  Is There a New Service Proletariat? The Tertiary Sector and Social Inequality in Germany. in G. Esping-Andersen (ed): *Changing Classes: stratification and Mobility in Post-Industrial Societies.* SAGE Studies in International Sociology 45.
Boje, Thomas (1991)
  'Mobilitet og strukturproblemer på det danske arbejdsmarked', *Dansk sociologi,* 2 (3): 35-53.

130

Boyer, Robert (1988)
The Search for Labour Market Flexibility. Oxford: Clarendon Press.

Bruun, Henry (1938)
Den faglige arbejdsbevægelse i Danmark. København: Instituttet for Historie og Samfundsøkonomi.

Carlos, Maria Leonor Palma & Genoveva Calvão Borges (1995)
The prevention of Racism in the workplace in Portugal. European Foundation for the Improvement of Living and Working conditions: Dublin.

Carroll, Glenn & Karl Ulrich Mayer (1986)
Job-shift patterns in the Federal Republic of Germany: The effects of class, industrial sector and organizational size. *American Sociological Review,* 51: 323-341.

Castells, Manuel (1989)
The Informational City. Information Technology, Economic Restructuring, and the Urban-Regional Process. Blackwell: Oxford.

Christoffersen, Mogens Nygaard (1996)
Opvækst med arbejdsløshed - En forløbsundersøgelse af to generationer født 1966 og 1973. SFI rapport 96: 14.

Cohen, Robin (1987)
The "New" International Division of Labour: A Conceptual, Historical and Empirical Critique. *Migration - A European Journal of International Migration and Ethnic Relations.* Bd. 1: 21-46.

Commons, John Rogers et al. (1918)
History of Labour in the United States. New York: Macmillan Co (4 vols.).

Courault, B. (1995)
Immigration and Labour Markets in Europe, XV Conférence de l'IWPLMS, Siène.

Cowell, Frank Alan (1990)
Cheating the Government: The Economics of Evasion. MIT Press: Cambridge.

Cyrus, Norbert (1994)
Flexible Work for Fragmented Labour Markets. The Significance of the New Labour Migration Regime in the Federal Republic of Germany. *Migration - A European Journal of International Migration and Ethnic Relations.* 6: 97-125.

Dahlgaard, Frank (1983)
Den sorte økonomi. *Samfundsøkonomen,* 1983, nr. 2: 8-24.

Doeringer, Peter B. & Michael J. Piore (1971)
International Labour Markets and Manpower Analysis. Lexington, MA: Heath.

Due, Jesper, Jørgen Steen Madsen & Carsten Strøby Jensen (1992)
EF & den sociale dimension. En sociologisk analyse. Jurist- & Øko-nomforbundets Forlag, København.

Due, Jesper, Jørgen Steen Madsen & Carsten Strøby Jensen (1993)
Den danske model - En historisk sociologisk analyse af det kollektive aftalesystem. Jurist- og Økonomforbundets Forlag, København.

Erickson, Christopher L. & Sarosh Kuruvilla (1994)
Labour Costs and the Social Dumping Debate in the European Union. *Industrial and Labour Relations Review*, Vol. 48, no. 1 (October 1994).

Erikson, Robert & John H. Goldthorpe (1985)
'Are American rates of social mobility exceptionally high? New evidence on an old issue', *European Sociological Review*, 1: 1-22.

Erikson, Robert & John H. Goldthorpe (1992)
The Constant Flux. A Study of Class Mobility in Industrial Societies. Oxford: Clarendon Press.

Esping-Andersen, Gøsta (ed) (1993)
Changing Classes. Stratification and mobility in post-industrial societies. London: Sage.

Feige, Edgar L. & R.T. McGee (1989)
Sweden's Laffer Curve: Taxation and the Unobserved Economy. *Scandinavian Journal of Economics* 85: 4, 499-519.

Flanagan, Robert J. (1993)
European Wage Equalization Since the Treaty of Rome. In Lloyd Ulman, Barry Eichengreen, and William T. Dickens, eds., *Labour and an Integrated Europe.* Washington, DC: Brookings Institution: 167-87.

Flora, Peter (1976)
Modernisierung und die Entwicklung der westeuropäischen Wohlfarts-staaten. Habilitationsschrift, University of Mannheim.

Friedman, Jonathan (1974)
Marxism, structuralism and vulgar materialism. *Man*, n.s. 9: 444-69.

Geiger, Theodor Julius (1948)
Klassesamfundet i Støbegryden. København: Gads Forlag.

Giddens, Anthony (1973)
The Class Structure of Advanced Societies. London: Hutchinson.

Glasser, William (1972)
Skolen uden tabere. Gyldendals pædagogiske bibliotek. Translated from *Schools without failure.* New York, London: Harper & Row 1969.

Godelier, Maurice (1966)
Rationalité et irrationalité. Paris: Maspéro.

Hadjimichalis, Costis (1986)
Uneven development and Regionalism: State, Territory and Class in Southern Europe. London: Croom Helm.

Haller, Max (1989)
Klassenstrukturen und Mobilität in fortgeschrittenen Gesellschaften.
Frankfurt a.M.: Campus.
Hjarnø, Jan (1976)
Migration fra Vest Samoa til New Zealand. I: *Den Ny Verden.* 10. årg.
nr. 3: 74-105.
Hjarnø, Jan (1980)
Social Reproduction. Towards an understanding of aboriginal Samoa.
Folk. Vol. 21/22: 73-123.
Hjarnø, Jan (1989)
Synet på arbejdsløse. Ungdomsbilleder i Esbjerg, delrapport 6. Sydjysk
Universitetscenter.
Hjarnø, Jan (1991)
Migrants and refugees on the Danish labour market. *New Community.*
Vol. 18: 75-87.
Hjarnø, Jan (1995)
Preventing racism at the workplace. The Danish National Report.
Working paper nr. WP/95/42/EN. European Foundation for the
Improvement of Living and Working Conditions, Dublin.
Hjarnø, Jan (1996)
*Global cities in two ways. A comment on Saskia Sassen's global city
hypothesis.* Papers, Migration No. 19. Danish Centre for Migration and
Ethnic Studies. Esbjerg: South Jutland University Press.
Hoffman, Henrik (1996)
Større ulighed giver lavere vækst. Arbejderbevægelsens Erhvervsråd,
Journal 0203/HH.
Homans, George Caspar (1961)
Social behaviour: Its elementary forms. New York: Harcourt.
Hovedstadens Statistikkontor (1994), Københavns bydele, Tal nr. 5/1994.
København.
Hovedstadsregionens Statistikkontor (1993)
*Arbejdspladsprognose 1991-2010 for kommuner og amter i hoved-
stadsregionen.*
Højrup, Thomas (1983)
Det glemte folk. Livsformer og centraldirigering. Hørsholm.
Højrup, Thomas (1995)
Omkring livsformanalysens udvikling. København: Museum tuscala-
num.
Illeris, Sven (1990)
Den regionale erhvervsfordeling i 1980'erne. AKF: Copenhagen.
Illum, Knud (1964)
Kollektiv Arbejdsret. København.

Industriel dynamik og regional inerti. *Ledelse & Erhvervsøkonomi* 53: 3: 139-149.

Ingemann, Hans-Jørgen & Jens Lind (1995)
Unges arbejde inden for handel og butik. Institut for Social forhold, Aalborg Universitet: Aalborg.

Iori, I. & Giovanni Mottura (1988)
Stranieri in agricoltura. I Cocchi, C., op.cit.

Isachsen, Arne Jon & Steinar Strøm (1980)
The Hidden Economy: The Labor Market and Tax Evasion, *Scandinavian Journal of Economics* Vol. 82: 304-11.

Isachsen, Arne Jon & Steinar Strøm (1981)
Skattefrit - svart sektor i vekst. Universitetsforlaget: Oslo.

Jacobsen, Per (1987)
Kollektiv Arbejdsret, København. Jurist- og Økonomforbundet.

Jensen, Peter; Jan Beyer Schmidt-Sørensen & Nina Smith (1992)
Kan arbejdsløsheden i Danmark afskaffes? *Fremtidsorientering.* 1, marts 1992.

Jeppesen, Hans-Jeppe & Lind, Jens (eds) (1991)
Changes in labour market and industrial relations in Europe. Ålborg.

Jepsen, Gunnar Thorlund (1994)
Is there Aversion against Moonlighting? Memo 1994-19. Institut for Nationaløkonomi og Statistik, University of Aarhus.

Kern, H. & M. Schumann (1984)
Das Ende der Arbeitsteilung? Munich: C.H. Beck.

Kuznets, Simon (1955)
Economic Growth and Income inequality, *American Economic Review,* no. 45: 1-28.

LABOS (1991)
Politiche sociali e bisogni degli immigrati. Rome.

Levy, Frank & Richard J. Murnane (1992)
U.S. Earnings Levels and Earnings Inequality: A Review of Recent and Proposed Explanations. *Journal of Economic Literature,* 30: 1333-81.

Lind, Jens (1994)
Arbejdsløshedspolitik i Norden - integration til hvad og hvordan? *CID studies no. 2.* Copenhagen Business School.

Lind, Jens (1995)
Trade Unions in a Changing Society. *CID studies no. 14.* Copenhagen Business School.

Lind, Jens & Ivar Hornemann Møller (1995)
Unemployment or Basic Income - is there a middle road? Copenhagen: CID, Centre for Social Integration and Differentiation, Copenhagen Business School.

Lipset, Seymour M. & Stein Rokkan, (1967)
Party systems and voter alignments: cross national perspectives. New York, London: Collier Macmillan.

Lundager, J. & Friedrich Schneider (1986)
The Development of the Shadow Economies for Denmark, Norway and Sweden: A Comparison. Memo 1986-1. University of Aarhus.

Madsen, Bent (1996)
Working poor. Arbejderbevægelsens Erhvervsråd. Journal 0203/BM.

Malheiros, Jorge Macaista (1996)
Foreign Workers in the Portuguese Labour Market: Examples of illegality and vulnerability. Paper presented for the International Seminar: Undocumented Immigrants on the Labour Market: Policy responses, Brussels 18-19 January.

Marx, Karl (1964)
Pre-capitalist economic formations. Eric J. Hobsbawn (ed), New York: International Publishers.

Mayer, Karl Ulrich & Walter Müller (1986)
The state and the structure of the life course, in A.B. Sørensen, F.E. Weinert and L. Sherrod (eds), *Human Development and the Life Course: Multidisciplinary Perspectives.* Hillsdale, N.J.: Lawrence Erlbaum Associates: 217-45.

Ministry of Finance (1995)
Finansredegørelse 1995.

Ministry of the Environment (1992)
Danmarks Byregioner - et atlas om de danske byregioners internationale muligheder. Copenhagen.

Müller, Walter (1985)
"Mobilitätsforschung und Arbeitsmarkttheorie", in: H. Knepel & R. Hujer (eds), *Mobilitätsprozesse auf dem Arbeitsmarkt.* Frankfurt a.M. & New York: Campus Verlag: 17-40.

Nayer, A. & M. Nys (1992)
Les migrations vers l'Europe occidentale. *Politique migratoire et Politique d'ontégration de la Belgique.* Foundation Roi Baudouin.

Nelleman, George (1981)
Polske landarbejdere i Danmark og deres efterkommere. København: Nationalmuseet.

Nielsen, Bue (1995)
Den regionale erhvervsudvikling i Danmark 1983-1993. Ministry of the Environment. Working Paper.

Nielsen, Ruth (1992)
Lærebog i Arbejdsret. Jurist- og Økonomforbundets Forlag.

Nielsen, Ruth (1995)
   Social rights and social welfare law discrimination perspective.
   Unpublished.
North, David S. (1993)
   Why democratic governments cannot cope with illegal immigration.
   The Changing Course of International Migration, OECD: 221-225.
OECD (1997)
   Employment Outlook.
Pedersen, Peder (1995)
   Kan det betale sig at arbejde? G.V. Mogenden (ed) Hvad driver
   værket? Copenhagen: Spektrum.
Pedersen, Peder J. & Nina Smith (1995)
   The welfare state and the labour market. University of Aarhus.
Pedersen, Søren (1991)
   Omfanget af den skjulte økonomi. Mimeographed. Institute of
   Economics, University of Copenhagen.
Persson, Torsten & Guido Tabellini (1994)
   Ulighed er skadelig for vækst. *The American Economic Review*, Vol.
   84, No. 3.
Petersen. J.H. (1994)
   Økonomien, økonomer og velfærdsstaten. *Nationaløkonomisk Tids-
   skrift.* Bd.132, 2.
Petersen, J.H. & J. Søndergaard (1994)
   *A Comprehensive Reform of the Income Transfer System. A recent
   Danish Proposal*, CHS Working Paper 1994:4, Odense universitet.
Piore, Michael J. (1979)
   Birds of Passage. Migrant Labour and Industrial Societies. Cambridge:
   Cambridge University Press.
Piore, Michael J. & Charles Sabel (1984)
   The Second Industrial Divide. New York: Basic Books.
Pires, Rui Pena (1993)
   "Immigration in Portugal. A typology Essay". *Recent Migration Trends
   in Europe* (ed. M.B. Rocha-Trindade). Universidade Aberta: Lisboa.
Plough, Niels (1994)
   The Welfare State in Liquidation? in Plough, N. & J. Kvist (eds) *Recent
   Trends in Cash Benefits in Europe, Social Security in Europe 4*,
   Socialforskningsinstituttet: København.
Plovsing, Jan (1994)
   Social Security on Denmark - Renewal of the Welfare State, in Plough,
   N. & J. Kvist (eds) *Recent Trends in Cash Benefits in Europe, Social
   Security in Europe 4*, Socialforskningsinstituttet: København.

Portes, Alejandro & Saskia Sassen-Koob (1987)
Making It Underground: Comparative Material on the Informal Sector in Western Market Economies. *American Journal of Sociology.* Vol. 93, no.1. July 1987: 30-61.

Portes, Alejandro & J. Walton (1981)
Labour, Class and the International System. New York: Academic Press.

Pyle, David J. (1989)
Tax Evasion and The Black Economy. 1989. London: Macmillan.

Qvortrup, Jens (1971)
Karl Marx' "An Sich"-Klassebegreb. En teorihistorisk studie. *Kurasje,* no. 4: 3-38.

Qvortrup, Jens (1993)
Gulerod og pisk. *Information* 17 September 1993, København. p 2.

Ramakers, Joan (1996)
Undocumented Immigrants on the Labour Market. Main Topics and Agenda Setting. Paper presented at the International Seminar "Undocumented Immigrants on the Labour Market", January 18-19, 1996, Brussels.

Rayback, Joseph George (1966)
A history of American Labour. New York: Macmillan.

Ricardo, David (1926)
The Principles of Political Economy and Taxation. London, Dent & Sons Ltd. Everyman's library. Science; no. 590. First published 1911.

Rocha-Trindade, Maria Beatriz (1993)
"Portugal: The New Framework of Migration Policies". *Recent Migration Trends in Europe* (ed. M.B. Rocha-Trindade). Universidade Aberta: Lisboa.

Sassen-Koob, Saskia (1983)
"Capital mobility and labour migration: the expression in core cities": in: R. Timberlake (ed), *Urbanisation in the world economy.* New York: Academic Press.

Sassen-Koob, Saskia (1984)
"The new labour demand in global cities" in: M.P. Smith (ed), *Cities in transformation.* Beverly Hills: Sage: 139-171.

Sassen-Koob, Saskia (1987)
"Issues of Core and Periphery: Labour Migration and Global Restructuring", in: J. Henderson & M. Castells (eds), *Global Restructuring and Territorial Development.* London: Sage.

Sassen-Koob, Saskia (1988)
The Mobility of Labour and Capital. New York: Cambridge University Press.

Scheuer, Steen (1996)
Fælles aftale eller egen kontrakt i arbejdslivet. Nyt fra Samfundsvidenskaberne: København.

Schierup, Carl-Ulrik (1993)
På kulturens slagmark - Mindretal og størretal taler om Danmark.
Esbjerg: Sydjysk Universitetsforlag.

Schneider, Friedrich (1986)
Estimating the size of the Danish Shadow Economy using the Currency Demand Approach. *Scandinavian Journal of Economics*, Vol. 88, 1986.

Stalker, Peter (1994)
The work of strangers: A survey of international labour migration, ILO: Geneva.

Summers, C. (1983)
Comparisons in Labor Law: Sweden and the United States. *Svensk Juristtidning* 1983: 589 ff.

Sundram, Filip (1995)
En tidsrækkeanalyse of den sorte økonomi. M.Sc. Thesis, Økonomisk Institut: University of Copenhagen.

Viby-Mogensen, Gunnar (1985a)
Forskning i sort økonomi - en oversigt. *Nationaløkonomisk Tidsskrift* 123: 1-19.

Viby-Mogensen, Gunnar (1985b)
Sort arbejde i Danmark. Studie nr. 9 fra Institut for Nationaløkonomi, Handelshøjskolen i København: Copenhagen.

Viby-Mogensen, Gunnar (1987)
Historie og økonomi. Samfundsvidenskabelige synsvinkler på dansk historieforskning efter 1970. Publikation nr. 21. Institut for Økonomisk Historie: University of Copenhagen.

Viby-Mogensen, Gunnar (1989)
Den skjulte økonomi. *Dagligliv i Danmark.* Bind 2. Copenhagen.

Viby-Mogensen, Gunnar (1990a)
Time Use on Paid but Untaxed (black) Activities. *Time and Consumption* (ed. Viby-Mogensen, G.) Danmarks Statistik: Copenhagen: 217-242.

Viby-Mogensen, Gunnar (1990b)
Do-it-yourself Work. *Time and Consumption* (ed. Viby-Mogensen, G.). Danmarks Statistik: Copenhagen: 195-216.

Viby-Mogensen, Gunnar (1992)
Hvad er "sort arbejde", og hvad ved man om det? *Tidsskrift for Skatteret* 18: 523-527.

Viby-Mogensen, Gunnar (1994)
Forskning i den sorte sektor i Danmark 1980-92. Rockwool Fondens Forskningsenhed.

Viby-Mogensen, G., Hans Kurt Kvist, Eszter Körmendi & Søren Pedersen (1995)
The Shadow Economy in Denmark 1994. Measurement and Results. Danmarks Statistik: Copenhagen.

Wallerstein, Immanuel (1977)
"Rural Economy in World-Societies". *Studies in Comparative International Development.* 12 (Spring 1977): 29-40.

Weber, Max (1905)
The protestant Ethic and the spirit of Capitalism. Tranl. by Talcott Parsons. London: Allen & Unwin.

Åberg, Rune (1989)
Politik för jämlikhet - det goda samhällets huvudsak eller bisak? Dep. of Sociology, University of Umeå.

Author Index

Institutions and Company Index

Subject Index

144